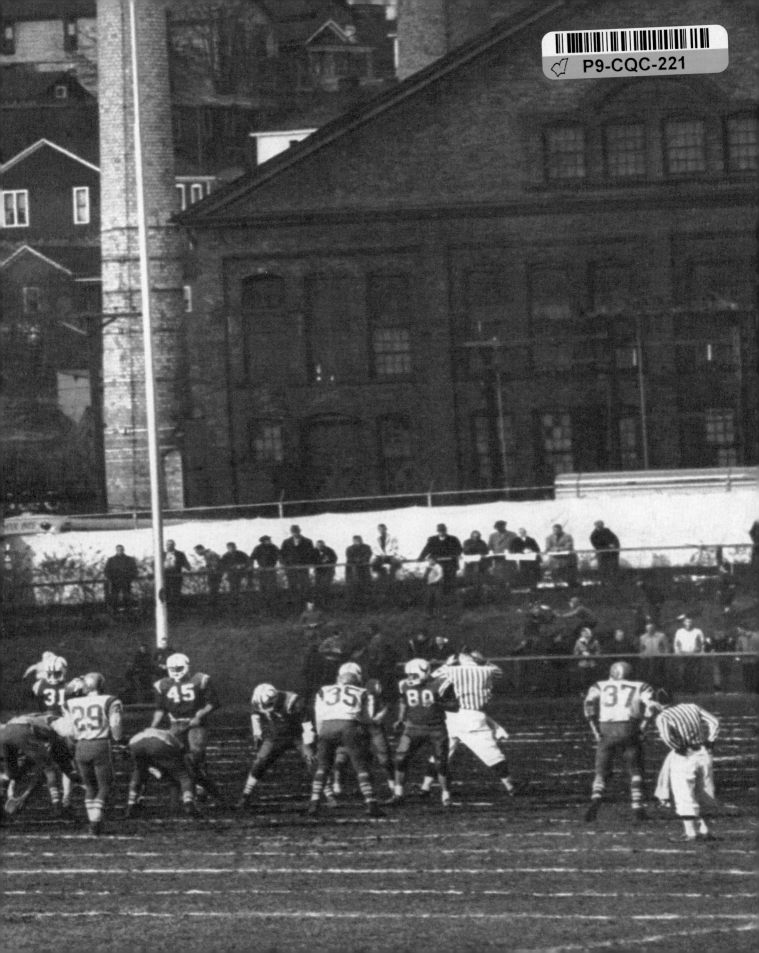

RUGGED LAND | 401 WEST STREET · SECOND FLOOR · NEW YORK CITY · NY 10014 · USA

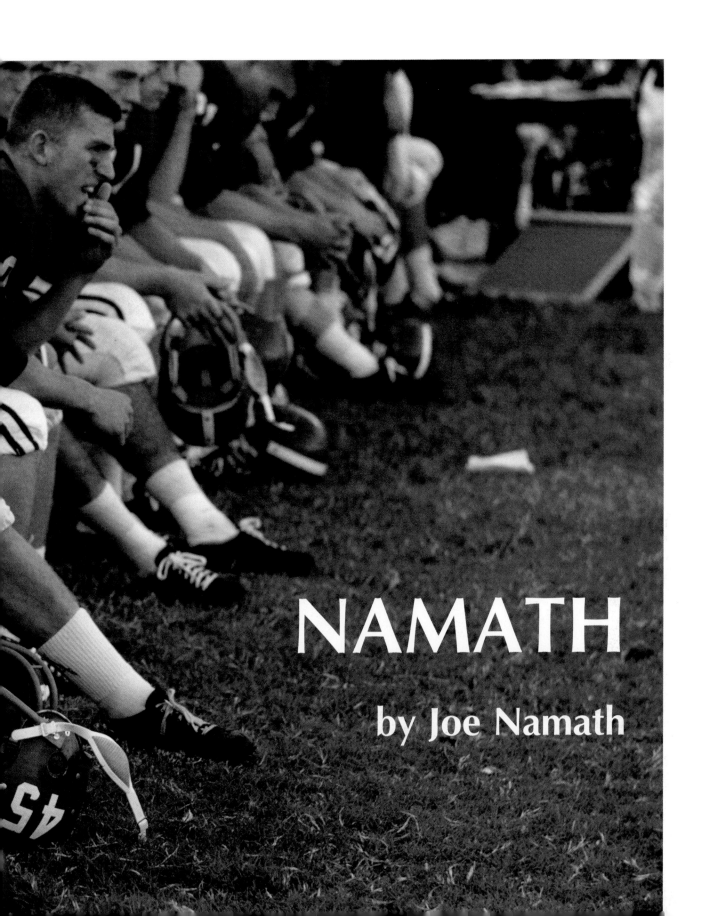

NAMATH

by Joe Namath

Published by Rugged Land, LLC

401 WEST STREET · SECOND FLOOR · NEW YORK · NY · 10014 · USA

RUGGED LAND and colophon are trademarks of Rugged Land, LLC

LIBRARY OF CONGRESS CATALOGING-IN-PUBLICATION DATA

Namath, Joe Willie, 1943-
Namath / by Joe Namath -- 1st ed.

p. cm.

ISBN-13: 978-1-59071-081-4 (hardcover)
ISBN-10: 1-59071-081-9 (hardcover)

1. Namath, Joe Willie, 1943-
2. Football players--United States--Biography.
3. Quarterbacks (Football)--United States--Biography.
I. Title.

GV939.N28A3 2006
796.332092--dc22

Book Design by
JK Naughton Design

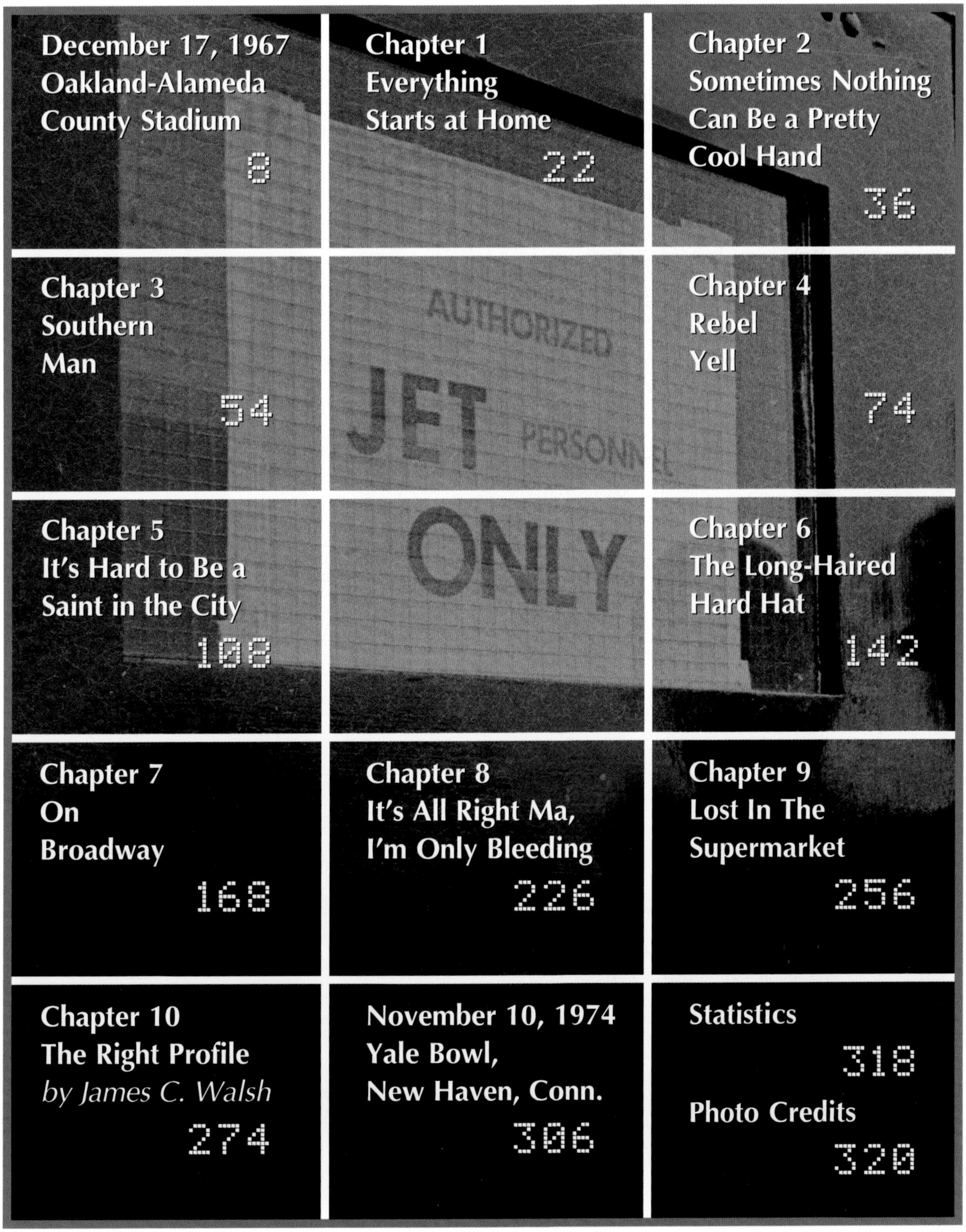

December 17, 1967
Oakland-Alameda
County Stadium
8

Chapter 1
Everything
Starts at Home
22

Chapter 2
Sometimes Nothing
Can Be a Pretty
Cool Hand
36

Chapter 3
Southern
Man
54

Chapter 4
Rebel
Yell
74

Chapter 5
It's Hard to Be a
Saint in the City
108

Chapter 6
The Long-Haired
Hard Hat
142

Chapter 7
On
Broadway
168

Chapter 8
It's All Right Ma,
I'm Only Bleeding
226

Chapter 9
Lost In The
Supermarket
256

Chapter 10
The Right Profile
by James C. Walsh
274

November 10, 1974
Yale Bowl,
New Haven, Conn.
306

Statistics
318

Photo Credits
320

Other Titles by Joe Namath

I Can't Wait Until Tomorrow...'Cause I get Better-Looking Every Day
(with Dick Schaap)

A Matter of Style
(with Bob Oates, Jr.)

Football for Young Players and Parents
(with Bob Oates, Jr.)

Dedication

Most of us who have lived the sport of football have continued to use its life lessons. Football has helped me foster determination within myself that has strengthened my desire to overcome adversity throughout this beautiful life.

It is with profound gratitude that I would like to dedicate this book to the leaders in my life—my family, my coaches and my teammates without whose guidance I might still be dreaming of professional baseball and shooting pool at The Blue Room.

I would also like to dedicate this book to my daughters Jessica and Olivia, the shining stars in my life. I love 'em.

Joe

Sunday, December 17, 1967
Oakland-Alameda County Stadium

New York Jets at Oakland Raiders

We just dropped two games at Shea Stadium, first to Denver and then Kansas City. Outsiders pointed in one direction to take the blame. Me. Even though the 1967 Jets and Houston Oilers shared first place in the AFL's Eastern Division Championship race, the media sold the "Joe Namath...all sizzle, no steak" story. Again.

Head coach Weeb Ewbank got us out of New York the day after the KC loss. The sooner we got on our California road trip and burned out the bitterness, the better. He made a big deal out of leaving a few days early for pre-game training in Santa Rosa (just north of Oakland in Sonoma) because of the weather, and then sprang two-a-day practices on us before we could begin to enjoy California. After all, we had to get ready for the nastiest bunch in the AFL, and some said all of football—Al Davis's Oakland Raiders.

The Raiders' record in their last fourteen games? 12-1-1. If it weren't for the New York Jets, they'd be 14-0-0.

Known as the Eleven Angry Men, the Raiders dominated on defense. And the molten core of that anger came from their defensive line. Two defensive ends, Ike Lassiter (6' 5", 278 lbs.) and Ben Davidson (6' 8", 272 lbs.), pinched offenses from the outside, while tackles Dan Birdwell (6' 4", 247 lbs.) and Tom Keating (6' 3", 268 lbs.) out-quicked most offensive linemen. They were coming into the game with a record 61 quarterback sacks in twelve games for losses of over 580 yards. But the sacks were just a fractional part of the pounding the Raiders gave quarterbacks.

In our day, there was no "in the grasp" rule (the whistle blows when the quarterback is in the grasp of a defender, put into the rule book in 1979) or running into the quarterback rule. And bump-and-run coverage was legal all over the field. Defensive backs were allowed to hit receivers until the ball was in the air, unlike today, where they can only "bump" once in the first five yards of scrimmage (this rule was put into effect in 1978). Before 1978, if you were a quarterback, defenses could run into you, hit you and take you down after you'd thrown the ball. Nowadays, any headshot to the quarterback or hitting and driving the quarterback into the ground is considered unnecessary roughness.

So it was not abnormal to get creamed after you threw the ball. You knew it was cheap. You knew it was late. So did the defense. But if the referee didn't call it, and he rarely did, all you could do was curse out the tackler and move on. The Raiders hit late— every chance they had.

So the Raiders must have been drooling after they watched the Jets-Chiefs game films from the previous week. Buck Buchanan (6' 7", 279 lbs.) and Ernie Ladd (6' 9", 302 lbs.) sacked me five times. Ladd said, "[Namath] was in pain… He came up limping and you could see it." Our battered running game must have given them confidence, too. Against the Chiefs, halfback Emerson Boozer tore cartilage and a ligament in his right knee on a freak hit. He was out for the

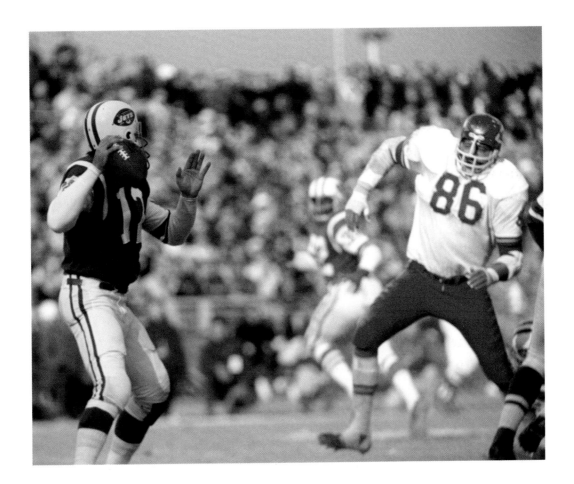

year. And fullback Matt Snell was just coming back after cartilage surgery on his right knee from a game against the Buffalo Bills in week two.

"Joe's a marked man. Joe knows it. We know it," said Dan Birdwell. Birdwell was a real character. I've heard he once tied one on the night before a game with the Broncos and then vomited all over the ball on the first play from scrimmage. He used to say, "I play like somebody just hit my mother with a two-by-four." Fun guy.

Tom Keating's sentiments were not so different: "What I love is to come in and reach out with an arm when the quarterback doesn't see you, he's not expecting it…he [goes] phuuuuh. That's fun, sure." I grew to like Tom.

And as for Ben Davidson, the NFL actually added a rule because of him:

A defender is prohibited from running or diving into or throwing his body against or on a ball carrier who falls or slips to the ground untouched.

Unfortunately, the "Ben Davidson" rule didn't go into effect until 1976. Davidson told the press, "This is the game we've been looking forward to all

year." Winston Hill, our outstanding left tackle, who protected my blind side, put it this way: "There are rough guys and there are dirty guys. Davidson's in a class by himself."

Ike Lassiter didn't say a word. He just wreaked painful havoc.

On Saturday, the Oilers beat the San Diego Chargers. Now we had to win just to keep pace. I found out later that Weeb's job depended on a Jet win, too. He had promised the Jets' owners (the Gotham Football Club, Inc.) a championship in five years. 1967? Year five.

Draped over a concrete wall, a black and white sign greeted us as we entered Oakland-Alameda Coliseum. "Classy Ben, Get Sassy Joe." Even the fans knew the Raider game plan. And what a pleasant group they were, too.

In the first half, our defense stuck them hard and our offense stayed with our blocks. The offensive line beat back their rush, time and time again. The Eleven Angry Men didn't get to me once…while I had the ball. I hooked up with the wily flanker Don Maynard for a score early. The 29-yard "60G Max " pattern put us on the board first. The term 60G meant that our two wide outs would run deep routes down their respective sidelines, Maynard on the strong side of the defense, George Sauer on the weak. The max call would tell Mathis and Snell, our backs, to stay in for maximum pass-protection blocking and would also let our line know that they had help if the Raiders blitzed. Pete Lammons, our tight end, ran a post pattern up the middle of the defense to pull safety coverage away from Maynard and Sauer. If Pete didn't hold a safety, I'd go to him. We executed the 60G beautifully, Maynard beat his man, and we had six.

On our first drive in the second quarter, I picked up a touchdown with my own two feet. We were a yard or so from their goal line after a nice long drive of close to 70 yards. Matt Snell took the ball on a P10 dive play, right up the gut. Matt tore right in between the center and the guard on our right-hand side

of the line. Boom! A linebacker's helmet knocked the ball square out of his hands. That sucker just squirted perfectly, straight back on one bounce into my hands. Two quick steps and a dive into the end zone, and I'm cradling the ball in the fetal position, untouched. Raider middle linebacker Dan Connors stood over me, trembling and screaming. Lying there securely in the end zone, looking up and seeing the look on Dan's face and hearing his tirade is still a wonderful memory.

Of all the games I ever played, that was the easiest, most fun touchdown I ever had. At the half, we were ahead 14-10.

Early in the third quarter, it's third down and 6 from our 21-yard line. I send split end George Sauer on a 15-yard curl pattern underneath weak-side cornerback Willie Brown and behind weak-side linebacker John Williamson. Because there are an odd number of players on each side of the line of scrimmage (eleven), the weak side of the field is usually determined by the position of the offensive tight end. If our tight end Pete Lammons is on the right side of the offensive line (as he was in this case) and we do not send anyone in motion to the other side of the line, then the right side of the offensive line is the strong side and the left side is the weak. More men on one side is "strong," while less men on the other is "weak." Sauer usually lined up as our weak-side split end, and Maynard was our strong-side flanker.

I figured Williamson would cover the weak side flat—a rectangular area about 8 to 10 yards deep from the left offensive tackle Winston Hill. George would have lots of room to cut his pattern off in front of cornerback Brown, who was responsible for a deep route down the sideline, and behind linebacker Williamson, who was responsible for coming up to defend against a halfback catching the ball in the flat—at least enough yardage to move the chains. I was half right.

While dropping back to pass, I read the defense and confirmed that the strength of their coverage was to the right. They were doubled up on Maynard on that side, leaving George one-on-one with Brown on the left. So I turned to throw to Sauer on the left, and just as I was releasing the ball—that split-second when my body was most vulnerable—Ike Lassiter delivered a knockout forearm to my face. He bore down on me with a force so fierce that I have no memory of the impact. I was told Dan Birdwell piled on. Of course.

Oh, I got the pass off. But not all of it. The ball didn't have as much speed on it as it normally did, thanks to Lassiter's hit. However, with my instinctive "feel" of having company—Lassiter was fast approaching—I might have thrown it a split-second early.

Now, a quarterback and a receiver spend about 120 hours and throw more than 7,000 passes a preseason (plus an hour or so every practice in season) to perfect their timing. George was trained for a ball from me at about 60 miles per hour on a curl pattern. And at 60 mph, the ball is fast enough to get to George before a linebacker or a defensive back can make a break on it and intercept it. But the Lassiter hit probably took a good 10 miles an hour of speed off that ball, so weak-side linebacker Williamson was able to make an easy break on the ball in front of George and got the interception. The turnover set up a Raider touchdown. They took the lead, 17-14.

When I got up, I didn't feel much pain, just otherworldliness. For me, the thing about a hit to the head (a concussion) is that after an initial gold flash…boom! There's a time lapse…seconds, minutes, whatever. Then a foggy calm follows. The body and mind filter out nonessential information—like what happened before you got hit, what might happen if you get hit again, what your mother's name might be. The mind focuses only on what's happening in the moment. For me, in that moment, this basic survival instinct is critical and naturally intertwines with years of training and habit. My body and mind ignore the noise, and I play from a place inside myself, kind of like being on autopilot. I'm not in complete control, my cognizance has waned, but I have access to basic memories, like certain plays. They just might not be the right ones for the particular team we're playing.

It's not like remembering a dinner date either, more like remembering a phone number. You don't know why you remember the phone number, you just do. And when the concussion fades, you can't exactly remember playing each play. You just feel like you did. You're kind of spaced out.

I walked over to the sidelines with the help of our center John Schmidt. I remember telling Dr. Nicholas that my face felt weird. I don't remember what he said in reply.

I also don't remember how the guys on the sidelines or in the huddle reacted to the hit. I was conscious of being there, but not all that aware of others being there with me. The Associated Press reported the next day that I was spitting blood. No big deal. At one time or another, someone on the field is spitting blood.

With 11:43 left in the fourth quarter, we got the ball back on our own 12. We had some offensive weapons, to be sure. We had two of the best receivers in the league (Maynard and Sauer) and a sure-handed bull in tight end (Pete Lammons). But without Boozer, and Snell running a 102-degree temperature (he picked up the flu on the way out to California), our running game just never got going that day. Even though the Raiders had just one sack—a meaningless 14-yard loss in the third quarter by Tom Keating—they held a solid lead at 24-14 (a touchdown followed after another Jet turnover). Now it seemed that everyone in the world knew that we had to throw on basically every down. A one-dimensional offense is in trouble.

I dropped back, nothing there. I rolled to my right, trying to find anyone with a white shirt on. I threw it away instead, into the flat, incomplete. But as my right arm came down on the follow-through, Ben Davidson came from behind me, on my blind side, with forearms at helmet height. He "sold out" on me—what we used to call unloading all of your momentum and force into another body. It's like when a baseball player hits a ball right on the meat of the bat. He knows instantly that he has all of the laws of physics working his way. Except in football, the quarterback is the baseball and the defensive player is the bat. Davidson got all of it, knocking my helmet clean off— flying 10 yards away from my head.

"I didn't know how much more the guy could take," Birdwell said after the game. "He looked right at me and grinned and said something, but he could have been talking in a foreign language."

Davidson received a roughing the passer penalty. His acceptance speech later: "I guess you got to get called for it, if you hit a guy in the face." The referee marched off 15 yards and signaled a Jet first down. Then he stopped the clock for an injury time out. People told me later that I lay facedown for longer than a boxer's ten count, but I didn't buy that.

Now, the one man who always looked after me was Jet center John Schmidt. Someone found my helmet and gave it back to me. John helped me up and I began walking to the wrong sideline. He corrected me and took me back to the huddle.

I guess I'd played with concussions before. They are an occupational hazard. I'd already been playing most of the game in a bit of a fog from Lassiter's hit, anyway. What are you gonna do? I called another pass. We lost 38-29.

Coach Bryant once said, "There's a difference 'tween bein' beaten and losin'." I agree. Now, I've been beaten in my life. Sure. But knowing the *difference* between being beaten and losing is something to be respected.

Later that night—Jim Hudson on crutches after he dislocated his hip in the game, Big Boy Pete Lammons, Curley Johnson and me with my black eye—picked up and went to Vegas for our day off.

The next day the papers reported that Ben Davidson had shattered my cheekbone in the fourth. But it had actually been Lassiter in the third.

"I didn't take no beating, I got my face swollen biting into a steak at breakfast," I said. I wouldn't give any opponent the satisfaction of knowing he hurt me. If you can't take it, don't play. It's a hard game.

by Joe Namath

CHAPTER 01 | Everything Starts at Home

The Lower End
Beaver Falls, Pennsylvania

I grew up in Beaver Falls (about 28 miles northwest of Pittsburgh), where most everyone was from somewhere else. We had Greeks, Irish, Germans, Italians, Polish, Czechs, Hungarians, Croatians, Serbians, Syrians, Blacks, Mexicans, Hispanics, and just about everyone else. English was pretty much

every kid's parent's second language. Only a few people had their noses in the air—a doctor here and a lawyer there, or a car dealer. They lived up on the hill in Patterson Heights. And even they worked hard. Hard work was just a given.

The same could be said about the way of life for the rest of our sports rivals in Western Pennsylvania—the likes of Aliquippa, Ambridge, Farrell, Midland, Butler, New Castle and Sharon. All formidable foes on the athletic field.

My dad, John Namath (Hungarian name Janos Nemet) of Raho, Hungary, stepped onto Ellis Island at eleven years old. And my mom, Rose Juhasz (Rosal), was the daughter of two off-the-boat Hungarians. Like everyone else who settled in Beaver Falls, my family came to the Pittsburgh area for work. They got plenty of it.

The spine of this country was built in Western Pennsylvania's steel mills. Our mills skirted the Beaver River and the Pennsylvania Railroad. My dad worked as a helper on a hot furnace at Moltrup Steel Company in his early twenties before landing a roller job on Hot Mill #2 at Babcock & Wilcox. He kept that job for the rest of his 51-year career. Someone once described Pittsburgh in the '40s as "hell with the lid off."

When I was eleven, my dad took me through the steel mill. I don't know why they allowed kids to walk through back then, but I'm glad they did.

Someone called out, "Hey John, that your boy?"

My dad nodded. "Yeah, showing him around." Working in the mill was hell with the lid on. He wanted me to see and feel it early.

Just about every dad and most brothers in Western PA worked at one of the mills. You'd see them shuffling off in the morning, with their lunch pails and ball caps. They'd finish work, even the graveyard shift, and get together for a shot of whiskey and a beer—an Imp and Iron (Imperial whiskey and Iron City beer). I used to wonder how they'd work the 11 p.m. to 7 a.m. shift and go to the bar at 7:15 a.m. and drink beer. But to them, it was a ritual. You didn't finish the work day until you downed that old boilermaker. They'd be a little grayer from the slag ash and exhausted, but proud of a hard day's work, sacrificing and earning for their families. You had to make ends meet. Then you tried to get ahead.

Now most of the mills are gone. But back then, there weren't many restrictions on the kind of junk you could pump into the air or into the river, either, and men like my father didn't object to what were clearly unsafe and life-threatening work conditions. But back home, men just didn't complain like that. Men shoulder the burden and press forward.

The mill gave them an emotional mix of pride in their work and a shared anger at being exploited. The truth was that mill workers, in my dad's time (1940s, '50s and '60s), raised families at low wages while breathing in garbage. They stood over 2,100-degree steel billets wearing long underwear to keep the constant heat off of their bodies, even as the summer temperatures soared outside. Different immigrant cultures worked side by side, shift after shift. They grew to respect one another by sharing a work ethic. You can't help respecting someone who shares the same burdens you do. So superficial differences—like a guy's skin color, funny accent, too much hair or lack of hair—burned away, forging a unique American community.

But hey, we had our share of jerks at home, too. Nevertheless, I learned from my mother, father, and brothers to stand by the people close to you—the people you believed in. It didn't matter who they were or where they came from.

It didn't take long, though, for a mill worker to get a chip on his shoulder. Eight hours a day, five days a week is a tough job anywhere. That kind of work tends to make a person think the world's unfair. It's no wonder parents aren't keen on seeing their children take their place in the mill.

So it makes sense that the game of football (which President Teddy Roosevelt threatened to make illegal because of a bunch of accidental deaths early in the century) took root in Western PA. Mill workers and coal miners formed football clubs, playing weekend games for civic pride. It wasn't long before people paid to see them play and—my goodness—even made a wager or two on the outcome.

In 1920 some businessmen in Canton, Ohio, met up in a garage (I'd say the NFL offices now, on Park Avenue, are a bit different) and decided to organize the various club teams into a professional league. The NFL's original franchises—Canton Bulldogs, Cleveland Indians, Dayton Triangles, Akron

Professionals, Massillon Tigers, Racine Cardinals, Decatur Staleys, Hammond Professionals, Rochester Jeffersons, Rock Island Independents and Muncie Goers—paid $100 (wow) to join the league and agreed to two core principles:

1) Not to sign players who are still in college

2) Not to steal each other's players (a saintly principle).

The two franchises that are still around today—the Decatur Staleys became the Chicago Bears and the Racine Cardinals, now the Arizona Cardinals—are worth hundreds of millions of dollars. Great sport, this football in America.

Pittsburgh joined the league in 1933 when the son of a North Side tavern owner, and perhaps the best pony handicapper of all time, Mr. Art Rooney, bought in for $2,000. Now, folks in Western Pennsylvania started living football even more than they had. Mr. Rooney was friendly with a New York bookmaker (legal at the time), Mr. Tim Mara. Mr. Mara started up the New York Giants in 1925 for $500, so Mr. Rooney thought a franchise that had quadrupled in value in less than ten years was a sound bet. Plus, Pennsylvania had just gotten rid of a small part of its Blue Laws, which would allow sporting events on Sundays. A good football game after church could become popular. Today, his team, the Pittsburgh Steelers, still packs them in after church.

Pro football was just part of the larger sports culture in Western PA. Mill workers, foundry workers, and country bumpkins too formed their own bowling leagues, bocce leagues, horseshoe, baseball, softball, football and basketball leagues. The men played a game, drank some beer and then went home for pierogies, goulash or kielbasa with the extended family. The boys began to catch on.

I spent all of my free time playing with some kind of ball—baseball, basketball, football—it didn't matter. Playing sports and watching games at one of the six baseball fields around town was what boys did in Beaver Falls. Trouble involved broken car windows and house windows or sneaking into gyms to play or watch a basketball game. And for a kid like me, with three older brothers and an older sister who had all been around the block, I had plenty of people insisting I behave.

Playing ball was nearly consuming for the young boy that I was. That's not to say I didn't know *something* about academics. Beaver Falls had a college. Aliquippa didn't have a college. Ambridge didn't have a college. We did! Geneva College was a source of pride for the people of our town, and it serenely sat on the hill at the north end. I dreamed of playing on its grass field—the Beaver Falls High School football team played home games there—but to my father, college offered an opportunity to stay out of the mills. My dad did not want his boys following him through the steel mill gate every morning, afternoon or night, and it was no secret that college scholarships were offered to kids who could play ball.

Some big-time football talent had come out of Western PA before I hit high school. Frank Sinkwich (1942), Johnny Lujack (1947), and Leon Hart (1949) won the Heisman Trophy. Beaver Falls players like Joe Walton and Jim Mutscheller made it to the pros and were on championship teams. Mike Ditka was an Aliquippa "Indian" and George Blanda, who played the game longer then anyone I ever heard of, had a coach at Kentucky named Paul "Bear" Bryant. And Rochester, PA's Vito "Babe" Parilli followed Blanda to Kentucky, became the Kentucky "Babe," and made all American.

When in first grade through seventh grade at St. Mary's School, at lunchtime I'd go see my mom, who was working at a five-and-ten store. It was about two blocks away, and I'd pass an Army Navy supply store on the way. There was a gold football helmet in the window made by Hutch, and had "Babe" Parilli's signature on it. I would stand and stare at that helmet just thinking, that if I was lucky, maybe, someday I might wear a similar helmet. Vito and I would share more history together down the road.

And hey, the men who have continued the Western PA tradition are something special too—Lavar Arrington, Fred Biletnikoff, Bruce Clark, Anthony Dorsett, Bill Fralic, Jim Kelly, Ty Law, Mike Lucci, Dan Marino, Joe Montana… Not bad for my short list.

Now, every kid football player in Western PA has a hero. As I grew older my football hero was Johnny Unitas.

And man, did Johnny U. have a story. He told it in his autobiography titled, simply, *Pro Quarterback*. The son of immigrant Lithuanian parents who grew up in Brookline, a stretch of row houses on the South Side of Pittsburgh, Johnny lost his father to pneumonia when he was just a boy. His mom took over the family's coal delivery business and worked nights cleaning office buildings in the city to keep the family afloat. John and his brother Len shoveled coal on the weekends and nights for 75 cents, while their two sisters, Millicent and Shirley, kept the house.

When high school came around, John weighed only 138 lbs., but he went out for the St. Justin's football team anyway. In his sophomore year, the starting quarterback broke his ankle. Johnny stepped behind center and never left. He beat out today's Steeler owner Dan Rooney for all-Catholic honors his junior year, and then made all-American his senior year.

Football gave him a shot at Notre Dame, where all Pittsburgh Catholic schoolboys dream of going. But after he worked out for Bernie Crimmins (ND's backfield coach) for a whole week, the Fighting Irish didn't think John was big enough. Just before the school year began, Johnny's high school coach, Max Carey, reached out to an assistant coach named John Dromo at the University of Louisville and landed his star a full scholarship.

The Cleveland Browns called him after his senior year at Louisville. They were going to pick him up late in the draft, but the Steelers beat them to it in the ninth round. Johnny thought he was set. He'd head back home, get married and make the Pittsburgh Steelers a contender.

The Steelers back then were pretty bad. The team was filled with veteran players who called Johnny "Clem Kadiddlehopper" behind his back (from a clown routine about a gangly hillbilly), and head coach Walt Kiesling cut him without letting him play a down. If not for a photo of Johnny showing a Chinese nun how to hold a football, he may have gone completely unnoticed. John hitchhiked home from camp to save the bus fare.

Writer Roy Blount, Jr. told a great story about Johnny in his book *Three Bricks Shy of a Load.* The only people in camp who said he was any good were two ball boys, young Rooneys, who wrote a 22-page letter to Mr. Rooney detailing just how good Johnny was. Mr. Rooney read it, but one of his cardinal rules was not to interfere with his coach's decisions. One day, Mr. Rooney was riding in his car with Coach Kiesling. He saw Johnny on the street, stopped his car, leaned over Kiesling in the passenger seat and said, "I hope you become the greatest quarterback in football."

Unitas spent that fall living with his in-laws, waiting on baby number two and working as a monkey man on a pile driver to make ends meet. On weekends he made an extra $6 playing semipro ball for the Bloomfield Rams. Then in February 1956, Johnny got the call. Don Kellett, the general manager of the Baltimore Colts, explained that the new head coach, Weeb Ewbank, had heard about Johnny Unitas through the football grapevine. He offered him a slot on the roster and a $7,000 contract if he made the team.

Johnny Unitas made the Baltimore Colts one of the greatest football teams in history. And he gave scrawny Kadiddlehoppers like me hope that maybe someday I could do something like that too.

by Joe Namath

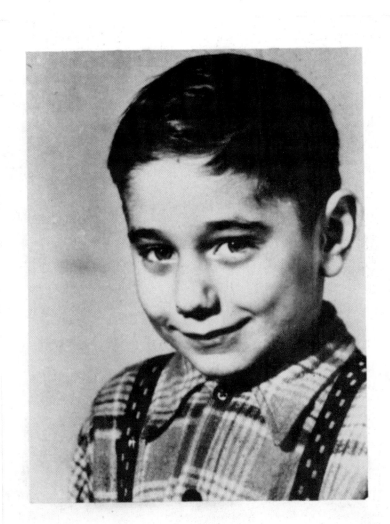

CHAPTER 02 | Sometimes Nothing Can Be a Pretty Cool Hand

The Blue Room/Bruno MBA

I don't think my mother or father ever consciously thought to themselves that they should push us boys into playing sports, but they did encourage us when we showed interest. Anything to get the kids out of the house was encouraged. But for them, sports were supposed to be played for enjoyment, and if they should lead to an education, all the better. If you played, though, you were to play your best. Games were a privilege, not a right.

My oldest brother, John Namath, Jr. (Sonny), was a terrific lineman who played alongside future Notre Dame star, and one of Johnny Unitas's prime targets, Baltimore Colt Jim Mutscheller. Sonny always had his heart set on a career in the military, though, and enlisted in the Army shortly after graduating from high school. He'd go on to serve honorably in both Korea and Vietnam.

My next brother, Robert Namath (Bob), was one heck of a quarterback. In fact, Brother Bob taught me how to throw a football from the ear shortening the throwing motion, a different technique then just throwing a stone or throwing a baseball. He drilled me from age six and taught me quite a bit of my coiled-torso throwing motion and emphasis on quick release. Bob was always a bit of a rebel and didn't finish high school, so he worked in the mill awhile, and then joined Sonny in the armed forces.

Frank, the third Namath, was Mr. Motivation. A lineman in football and a terrific catcher in baseball, Frank played on a full scholarship for Blanton Collier at the University of Kentucky. He played with an older guy named Lou Michaels,

who would end up with the Baltimore Colts. Frank took the scholarship without knowing he had received a bonus offer of $20,000 to join the Baltimore Orioles. My dad never told him. $20,000 was a lot of money back then, still is. But my dad didn't want Frank passing up college for money. Frank was not pleased when he found out about it, though. He loved baseball.

Frank was responsible for teaching me the importance of learning from a loss and how to be a gracious winner, with humility. You see, Frank is six years older than I am, and I'll tell you, if I had the good fortune of winning a game of stickball or electric baseball or something, I knew not to brag. I mean, not even a little smirk would be a good idea.

The thing about my sister Rita, who is Frank's age, is that it didn't take me long to learn a respect for how strong she is. She had to deal with those brothers too. And she joined our family when I was four. My parents had decided to have another child after Frank, and they were expecting a girl. Then I came along. Overjoyed with my presence, I'm sure, but still wanting a girl, my mom and dad adopted Rita. She was all of ten, with pigtails, and I hid in the corner when my mom brought her home.

As I grew—and I grew slowly—my best buddy Linwood Alford and I picked up some tricks here and there. We'd hustle empty bottles from people's back porches and take them down to the grocery store for the deposit money. We'd also go to the back of the junkyard and pull some stuff from under the fence. Then we'd go to the front and sell it back to Mr. Shamsky, who owned the yard. I mean, who did we think we were fooling? Mr. Shamsky? Nah, he was a nice guy who was all right with that a time or two. We would bring him legitimate stuff too, like scrap metal from the mills that we found near the river.

My mom wrote a book about our lives years ago, and she got a real kick out of Linwood's and my adventures. She called us Namath and Alford Enterprises. We had a ball, and I think my mom did too, watching us make our way through town. We were occasionally mischievous, but Linwood had older brothers too, and we pretty much toed the line. If we didn't, our big brothers would let us know very quickly.

It's probably hard to believe today because so many people go through it, but when two people got divorced in the 1950s in a place like Beaver Falls, it became something of a scandal. Children from "broken homes" would get sidelong glances, and neighborhood parents would tell their kids to steer clear of them. They were thought of as troublemakers, rabble-rousers not to be trusted. If the children had behaved themselves, the kids were told, the parents would still be together. That's the way some people thought back then about divorce.

Anyway, my mom and dad split up when I was in the seventh grade. With Sonny, Bobby, Frank and Rita out of the house by that time, we sold our house on Sixth Street and my mom and I found our first apartment on Twenty-Third Street. We had to walk up an outdoor wooden staircase to this single floor, two-bedroom apartment on the roof of a nightclub. Leaving the only home I'd ever known (a house with a backyard) was a pretty major move.

I had problems sleeping there. Bad dreams… I explained to my mother that it felt like things were on me when I was in bed. But every time I got up and turned on the light, there was nothing. So she came into my room and lifted up the mattress, and there were plenty of bugs…roaches! As soon as we could we moved away to another place on Thirty-Fourth Street, close to Geneva College—half of a two-family row-house. This is when I first started thumbing my way to and from school. A short while later, my mother met my stepfather-to-be and we moved to a house on Eleventh Street and Fourth Avenue. I went back to walking to school.

My mother worked hard and took pride in everything she did. She worked at W.T. Grant's as a buyer of clothes for the women's department and worked at another lady's shop in town too. On the side, she cleaned house for a doctor

up on the hill in Patterson Heights. The fact of the matter is that she always worked away from the house. And she always worked at the house. She didn't get much time off when I was still in the house, but I don't recall her complaining about it. Her actions spoke for her, and I grew to recognize, then respect the sacrifices she would make for her family and home.

Now, talk is cheap where I come from. If you're going to talk a game, you better be able to play it. The first time I heard that was from my brother Bob. I smarted off to him and he told me, "Talk is cheap and I'm gonna give you some change." And at that time he meant a good smack. You see, it's not what you say, but how you go about things. How you do it. Actions speak louder than any words you can say. I believe our actions mirror our makeup. So I was taught to obey and be humble. And I learned to be gracious and thick-skinned when it came to matters of winning and losing. If I wasn't, I had Bob and Frank to remind me. Believe me, my brothers always stayed close by. "Talk is cheap" is a good lesson to learn when you're young.

As a twelve-year-old, I thought status in the world was gained on the ball field or on the street. There was one way of being respected for being smart, and that was being street-smart. Kids who did well in class didn't get the girls on Saturday night. It was the ball players and the wise guys who got their names in the paper, not the kids with the straight A's. Now, I'm sure that wasn't true, but that's the way I felt at the time.

From the sixth grade on, a friend of mine named Richie Chido and I used to pray to Saint Jude (the Saint of Hopeless Causes, or what I like to think of as difficult tasks) to get taller. Our prayers hadn't kicked in yet by the time I started ninth grade. I was only about five feet tall and weighed about 115 lbs. Football season didn't look good for me. Plus, my buddy Jake Lotz was bigger, stronger and faster than me, and he was our starting quarterback. I don't remember how it happened, but Jake broke his hand. Like Johnny U., I got an opportunity and took advantage of it.

We only played five games that season (1957), but my mom and dad were proud that their youngest made the papers. The *Beaver Falls News-Tribune* called me the "pint-sized quarterback" who directed "one of the most devastating offenses for a junior high team witnessed in several seasons." I threw some touchdown passes and we won some games.

But my true loves then were basketball and baseball. A junior high school basketball coach from Ellwood City who also coached the town's high school football team said some really nice things about me when we played them. It was a man named Chuck Knox. I'd run into him a few more times down the road.

When I hit high school, I just about gave up on football. I knew I could play, and I'd had a good year in ninth grade, but the coaches put me as the fifth-string quarterback on the varsity. I was still a runt, and I didn't get invited to the Beaver Falls Booster Club varsity summer camp for the high school football team. When you're fourteen years old and your whole life is about trying to make the team, man, it was devastating.

When the team returned from camp, I told head coach, Mr. Bill Ross, I was going to quit. He asked me to stay. He told me that he'd been watching me play and that my brothers were good players before me. He said he thought that I could eventually play. That meant a lot to me, because I needed some encouragement. So I stayed on the team, albeit the fifth string. One of his assistant coaches, an older cranky gentleman named Leland Schackern, saw something in me too, and he took up where my brothers left off. He told me, "Namath, I'm going to make you a passer." Teaching me about different throwing speeds (touch), Mr. Schackern showed me how to take something off the ball and when to rifle a pass—how to deliver a ball that a receiver can handle. I only got in one game that year and it was at defensive back, but I moved from fifth-string to third-string quarterback by the end of the season. More importantly, I learned how to suck it up, bide my time and keep my head up.

Three days after Christmas that year, the man who knew how to suck it up better than most, led the Baltimore Colts over the New York Giants in an overtime to win the 1958 NFL Championship. Johnny Unitas made head coach Weeb Ewbank's wild promise to bring the Colts a championship in five years come true.

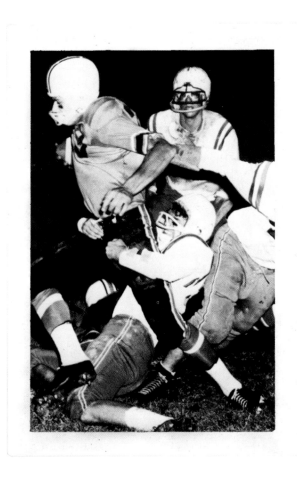

However, it took me a little longer to find some street smarts. There was a place to pick them up, alright—the Blue Room. Every town has one, or did back then: a joint where you could cut class, shoot a game of pool, smoke a cigarette, get into some friendly trouble and generally get your cool on. It was right on the main drag, Seventh Avenue, and there was a luncheonette in the front of the pool hall. You'd stride through the front and head to the back room and be greeted by a dozen gleaming Gold Crown Brunswick pool tables. Man, those tables were hot. Slate and felt was good on all of them.

One of the first times I walked in there, I got hustled out of some of my mother's hard-earned money. I was fifteen, sent on an errand to pick up a few things at the market. I had 35 cents of her change in my pocket, so I stopped at the Blue Room with the idea of turning that 35 cents into a couple of bucks. Well, I lost. My stomach was tossing and turning on the long walk home; I was near sick, just knowing that Mom would ask for the change. I wouldn't have it, and she'd tell my brothers what I'd done. She never asked! I spent more time worrying about it than that 35 cents was worth.

That was lesson one from the Blue Room. Don't put money on the table that's not yours.

In 1959, my junior year, Coach Ross was promoted to athletic director, and he brought in one of the best coaches in Western Pennsylvania to take over the Beaver Falls Tigers program. Coach Larry Bruno, lured from rival Monaca, just down the valley, graduated from Geneva College and was one heck of a player himself, selected to play in the all-star college East-West Shrine Game in California.

No matter how "cool" I thought I was hanging out at the Blue Room, the fact was that I was a fifteen-year-old kid from a mill town, who was not being motivated in school. I had at best a C average and thought that the wise guys who ran numbers on Seventh Avenue had all of the answers. What I needed most at this time in my life, though I certainly wasn't aware of it then, was for an outsider to let me know I had something special, someone who I admired and respected who did not have the last name Namath. Coach Bruno was that guy. He made the difference.

He wasn't condescending. He took the time to teach his players the skills. For me he focused on leadership, footwork and ball handling—skills that I used throughout my entire football career—and gave me the initiative to develop an athletic discipline. Linwood and I used to go to his house about three times a week during summer vacation to work on drops and pass routes. Granted, these sessions started as yard work. He had us cleaning up his backyard, and we'd start talking football. It soon led to him showing me something. In these sessions, which were on his own personal time, he taught me the correct footwork technique to make every step from point A to point B the most efficient. No wasted movements. He taught me how to properly fake a handoff, how to call a game, call an audible at the line, how to read game film, defensive formations—just about every quarterbacking fundamental. Plus, he got his yard cleaned up.

Coach Bruno was also a magician. Literally. And our offense developed his personality. We had the most deceptive ball handling in Western PA. It was so good that the officials would be stumped too. I remember playing New Castle, and the referee blew the whistle thinking the ball was in a running back's hands when I still had it going around right end on an option play.

For all of his encouragement, Coach Bruno didn't make me the starting quarterback my junior year. I'm not embarrassed to say that our starter, Rich Niedbala, was a better football player than I was. He'd go on to the University of Miami on a full football scholarship. The competition is so intense in Western PA that I've heard people call their high school third-stringers all-State Rhode Island.

Sadly, the 1959 season continued the tradition at Beaver Falls High. We finished 3-5-1, but we did win the coveted "Little Brown Jug," which was kept by the winner of the annual Beaver Falls/New Brighton rivalry. New Brighton was a class-A school located across the Beaver River, and while we usually won the game in my day, it was fun for me and the other reserves to get in there and play almost four full quarters. I ended up throwing three touchdown passes and ran one in too. It was a great head start for my senior year, but I don't think anyone in town expected what was to come in the following season.

Nineteen sixty was the football season that our town had never experienced. At that time, the highest caliber of high school football in Western Pennsylvania was "AA." And Beaver Falls had one of the lowest enrollments to get the AA status. Because we had fewer kids to draw from (just over the 1,000-student threshold), we *usually* ended up with a losing season. The team hadn't won any kind of title in over 32 years.

Our team was smaller than just about everyone else, and without much depth. But we had great coaching, some good quick players and the smarts and discipline as a team to run a sophisticated offense and defense. We were just hungry enough that the past didn't matter. I believe to this day Coach Bruno was ahead of his time. By stressing fundamentals of the game, the physics of it—how to properly block, tackle, throw, run, position yourself for the best possible outcome—he communicated these core truths in a way that we could understand. We bought into his program and believed we could win. He gave us confidence.

Coach Bruno also had some fine assistant coaches. Offensive line coach Gene Harr taught our smaller linemen how to out-quick the bigger guys in front of them. He taught them how to get position on them and trap them into being out of control, so that our running backs could pick through the carefully designed openings and break into the secondary.

Same thing went for our passing game. Coach Dan Sakaress taught our receivers how to be in the right place at the right time. He stressed the relationship between repetition and timing. The timing between the QB and receiver (the amount of time it takes for the receiver to get the ball in his hands after he makes his break) was tight, because we worked as close to full-out on every play in practice as possible. You will never be able to practice like you play in a game, because there are too many variables. But if you repeat plays over and over again and practice as if you are in a game situation, you can limit the time the receiver has to wait for the football after his break. That's called good timing.

If you add up the time that Coach Bruno spent with his quarterbacks to make sure that their passing footwork was efficient and as quick as possible, plus the hard work we put in to make our QB/receiver timing tight, and throw in the fact that I learned early on how to throw the ball from my ear, you can understand why we had success getting the ball away a fraction faster than the defenses may have expected. The margin of speed is a big deal, no matter what sport. But when your offensive line is smaller than the defensive line they are opposing, speed can be a huge deal. With this in mind, Coach Bruno taught us how smaller, quicker guys can beat bigger guys: by using the angles of the game and by using your brains.

Another positive factor that Coach Bruno brought to the team was the joy of the work. He loved it and helped us love it too. We were learning, getting better, and anxious to play.

We began the year in good style. We beat Midland 49-13 and Sharon 39-7. We then shocked a team we hadn't beaten in 30 years, New Castle, 39-0, and we prepared for Ambridge, a game that we knew was going to be a fight. We didn't like one another.

The Bridgers nailed me when I was running an option on the second play of the game. They separated my left shoulder, tearing one of the three ligaments that hold the shoulder in place. I sat out third down and came back fourth down to punt. They held us to just 14 yards of total offense late into the first half. We were losing 6-0 and we had the ball on about our own 45-yard line.

On third down, I sent our left end, Tom Krzemienski on a post corner route. It worked beautifully. Tom had left the DB thinking post, while I rolled right to pull the defense that way. I set up, looked back, and saw that Tom had beaten his man, so I let it go. He caught the ball on a dead run, and after converting the extra point we made it to the half with a 7-6 lead. The rest of the game we just out-classed them, and we came away with a 25-13 win. I only

hit on three of 15 passes, but at least one of them was for that touchdown to Tom. A bad stat game will always come in a distant second to a win.

Because of my shoulder separation, I couldn't practice for a few days, and we had to see a couple of doctors before my dad, Coach Bruno, and I found one sympathetic enough to let me keep playing. But we did. And the Beaver Falls Tigers finished out the year undefeated. For the first time in its history we won the AA Championship.

After the season, we were all high on ourselves. The college recruiters made us feel even more invincible. A lot of my teammates (Tom Krzemienski, Tony Golmont, Jim Seaburn, Bert Kerstetter, Stan Kondracki, Terry Krivak, Ernie Pelaia, Larry Patterson, Butch Ryan) ended up playing college football. I had offers in from several colleges and I was just overwhelmed. Some of them offered me some illegal money, along with a car, and that sounded great, but my brother Frank told me not to go to a school like that. "If you play for a cheat, you are a cheat." So I didn't.

On a recruiting trip to Miami University, I was with Tom Krzemienski, meeting with head coach Andy Gustafson. We were making small talk, and Coach Gustafson asked Tom how many brothers and sisters he had.

"Eight brothers," Tom said.

"Wow, that's a big family," said Coach Gustafson.

"And nine sisters."

"What! Heck, son, we ought to have your mother here! She must be a heckuva woman!"

At the end of all of the recruiting, I decided that if I was going to play football, I wanted to go to Maryland. They had an innovative coach named Tom Nugent (credited with developing the "I" formation). On my recruiting trip, I was greeted at the airport by Al "Hatchet" Hassan, a wonderful guy from New Castle who was on scholarship as the team's equipment manager and assigned to host my visit. He landed in Maryland after a stint in the Navy. Hatchet would become my lifelong friend. I signed a letter of intent to attend Maryland in the fall of 1961.

Al and I started working on my College Board scores. All I needed to do was improve those about ten points to get the "official" acceptance to the university. But as it were, I honed my verbal skills engaging young ladies in conversation while I perfected my math skills adding up the Seven and Sevens that I drank at a refined New Castle tavern.

When my scores came back, the Namath family was disappointed to learn that I had flunked. I didn't measure up. And failure never feels good.

CHAPTER 03 | Southern Man

Sweet Home Alabama

It was July of 1961. I was 17 years old, and I faced one of those decisions that could have a huge impact on the rest of my life. At the time, I didn't understand the importance of the situation. The decision was out of my hands, though. My mother and brothers were going to tell me what to do.

I thought I knew what I wanted to do. I was convinced I knew. But guess what? We don't always get to do what we want. As the youngest, I never questioned the family's right, power or expertise in making this decision. It turned out well.

At the time, though, it stunk.

Like my brother Frank, I played a lot of baseball and showed some promise as a prospect. Our Beaver Falls Team won the WPIAL AA baseball championship my senior year, and I ended up hitting .450. So with all the recruiting for football, I was also getting some feelers about joining a major league baseball team. One of the fellows I talked to about joining a major league team was none other than Tommy Lasorda. Every time we've been together since, we always talk about the Beaver falls days.

The Baltimore Orioles, who didn't land brother Frank, tried for another Namath, along with the Kansas City Royals, St. Louis Cardinals and the Chicago Cubs. Eventually, the bidding for my services went up to $50,000 from the Cubs. Plus my mother and father were not as successful keeping this a secret from me as they were with Frank.

Like it was yesterday, I remember the family meeting...my mom, Bob, Frank and me at the dining room table. Sonny and Rita were in the Army at the time. My brother Bob asked mom what she wanted Joey to do. Mom said, "Owwwwww, I want Joey to go to college." Bob slammed his fist on the table and said, "That's it. You go to college." I wonder if Frank wasn't rooting for baseball. Anyway, no questions asked. I was just a bit peeved.

With the fall fast approaching and my college board score keeping me from going to Maryland, I started thinking about that fifty grand and a powder blue white rag-top Oldsmobile and chewing tobacco in Wrigley Field for a living. But my mom and a coach from the University of Alabama, Howard Schnellenberger, were determined to get me to college.

Coach Schnellenberger had some history with the Namath family. He played football at the University of Kentucky and as a senior there, he knew my brother Frank. While both Frank and Coach Schnellenberger played for the legendary coach Blanton Collier that year (1958), it was Coach Paul "Bear" Bryant who had made Kentucky a football power. And Coach Bryant had done that with two Western PA quarterbacks—George Blanda and Vito "Babe" Parilli. Coach Bryant occasionally would share some of his experiences with his players. We once heard Coach say that he knew he didn't belong at the University of Kentucky after a year-end awards banquet. The school presented the head basketball Coach, Adolph Rupp, with the keys to a new Cadillac. They gave Coach Bryant a wristwatch.

When he told us, a big ol' smile broke out on his face and he said, "Shoot. I knew right then this was a basketball school. Wasn't ever gonna be a football school. I didn't belong there"

I learned a lot about Coach Bryant by reading his autobiography, *Bear: The Hard Life and Good Times of Alabama's Coach Bryant.* He was born in 1913—just about the same time as my dad. Raised in a place called Morrow Bottom, Arkansas, he was the eleventh of twelve children, three of which died in infancy. By working the 260 acres of the family's "truck farm," they ate what they could raise on their own and sold whatever was left. As a boy,

Coach Bryant had to get up at 4 a.m. every morning to hitch mules to a wagon and drive his family to the nearby town of Fordyce. His mother would sell produce from the truck while the children went to school.

A lot of their customers were black people, and he naturally befriended a number of them in the area. He just felt more comfortable with them than the white townspeople. Till his dying day, he never did forget all the insults those pampered white kids spat at him while he fed his mules during recess. "I was sensitive to any kind of putdown. At recess, I had to go out and feed the mules their oats and chops while everybody else played. I can still hear those giggly girls, enjoying my embarrassment. I haven't forgotten *their* names either."

What makes me smile now is that Coach Bryant used very distinctive terminology for his Crimson Tide offense. Instead of saying right and left, we'd say "Gee" for right and "Haw" for left. This is the language he used to guide his mules. It was new to me but familiar to all of my teammates. "Gee," the mule goes right. "Haw," and the mule goes left. I guess Coach figured if a mule could understand it, so could we.

When he hit the eighth grade, though, he found a way out from under the bottom, and it wasn't by fighting a bear on a carnival stopover in Fordyce. (That fight is how he got his nickname—one his players never addressed him by.) As he said in his autobiography, "All I had was football, and I hung on as though it were life or death, which it was."

The chip he'd grown on his shoulder from the days he spent pushing a plow through the heavy Arkansas soil made him one heck of a tight end with an attitude. He had a remarkable career at the University of Alabama, playing with Green Bay Packer Hall-of-Famer Don Hutson, and winning the 1934 National Championship. But it was one game in particular that would forever cement his reputation and one that would become the benchmark for all players after him.

The 1935 Crimson Tide, coming off its National Championship, stumbled badly at the beginning of its season. They were 1-1-1 going into their biggest game of the year against the Tennessee Volunteers in Knoxville. Young Paul Bryant had a broken leg, but he traveled to the game with the team and had the cast cut off the night before the game so that he could walk the sidelines. In one of the all-time great coaching psyche jobs, he was called out in the pre-game pep talk by Head Coach Frank Thomas and asked if he could play. He did. The team, so inspired by his leadership, thrashed the Vols 25-0.

When I was 18, though, I knew nothing about Alabama and had no knowledge of Coach Bryant. All I wanted to do was play professional baseball. Especially when there was the baddest Oldsmobile Starfire convertible with my name on it waiting for me at the local dealership. I knew I could kiss that Starfire goodbye, though, when Coach Schnellenberger showed up at our door. After little more then an hour, Mom went upstairs, came down with a packed suitcase, looked at Howard Schnellenberger and said, "Take him." I got myself together. You know, cap, cheaters, toothpicks, Mom gave me a few bucks, a hug and kiss, and I was gone.

The report that I got was that Maryland's Coach Nugent called Coach Bryant and told him I was still available. After that phone call Coach Schnellenberger did what Coach Bryant told him to do. He got on the first plane to Atlanta, then to Pittsburgh, and drove to Beaver Falls. I went back with him to Tuscaloosa that night.

Now, I didn't panic. I'd taken a few recruiting trips already so when my mother had the bag packed, there I was, almost a veteran of traveling. But I always came back home.

The first time George Blanda met Coach Bryant, George said, "This must be what God looks like." The first time I met with Coach Bryant was in the middle of a practice session. Coach Schnellenberger and I had just arrived,

and we were standing between a couple of practice fields when this voice came from above and said, "Howard." Coach Schnellenberger looked up at Coach Bryant standing in his tower and proceeded to understand what coach Bryant said. He turned to me and said, "Go on up there." I said, "What?" He said, "Go on up there. Coach Bryant wants to meet you." When I got to the top of the tower, we shook hands and I was taken aback by his dominating size and steel grey eyes. He would point to a player on the field sand say, "Etterboyastud." He'd point another place and say, "Erernottherboyastud." I tried to understand what he was saying, but I only understood the word "stud." And I didn't know what it meant.

Looking back, I think he had a sense of the kind of guy I was. He had coached George and Vito—two Western PA guys—and he got them to reach very high levels of play. Now knowing Coach Bryant and how he put pressure on people to grow, he brought me up to his tower for a reason—to put me on a stage. In front of my whole class of teammates, he was saying to them and to me, "Get a good look at the new pupil. Now it's up to him to own up, or get run off."

At the time, I didn't know the tower was a special place. And over the years, I've heard so much about it (I may have been the only player he ever took to the top of the tower) that it has stuck with me. Because he coached George and Vito before me, he knew the cut of man he was going to get from Western PA. And I think he rightly thought that the best way to get a Western PA player to perform was to put him in a position of stress. Make him prove himself. Make him fight. But, and this is a big *but*, he had to make it Coach Bryant's way or he had to leave.

Now, there are three things I learned very quickly during my first day in Tuscaloosa, Alabama. First, it was hot (late August) and second, it smelled just awful. At the time, Tuscaloosa had a paper mill. And that paper mill took some getting used to. It threw off a putrid smell. Oh, man. It was just sickening, and when you combined it with the heat and a full-pad football practice, it took real effort to keep from vomiting.

I did have previous training getting used to awful smells. In Beaver Falls, our home games were played at the Geneva College stadium, which sat right next to the Armstrong Cork Plant. Not only did that plant spew some nasty fumes, but when the wind blew just right, the exhaust blew onto the field.

The third thing about Alabama in 1961 was that it still lived in the Jim Crow era. Everything was segregated. I know that's no news flash to anyone who has gray hair, but for people who weren't around back then, it's hard to explain just how ridiculous it felt. It didn't make any sense to me.

To abide by NCAA recruiting regulations that would allow the Athletic department to pick up my plane fare to campus, I had to leave town after I visited Coach Bryant at the practice field. So I was driven to the Greyhound bus station to get a ticket to Birmingham, where I would stay with an Alabama alumnus for the evening. When I walked into that bus station, I saw signs above the water fountains labeled "white" and "colored." Then I got on the bus and took one of my normal seats toward the back.

The fellow who was meeting me got very concerned, because while he was waiting for me, all the white people got out, then the black people, and he thought I'd missed my bus. I just had a hard time putting segregation together in my head. I was naïve, ignorant. I just couldn't digest it.

On the way back to Tuscaloosa, on Route 11, crossing the bridge, to my right was a Ku Klux Klan meeting going on. And when you'd pass a town sign, where there would be welcomes from the various civic societies, there'd be a welcome from the local KKK.

I moved, like all the ballplayers did, into a separate athletic dormitory. And while freshmen were not permitted to play on the varsity squads back then, we did scrimmage with them and played three freshmen games. We beat Mississippi State and Tulane, but tied Auburn. I didn't have many problems with the offensive system; Coach Bruno's offense in Beaver Falls was more sophisticated than Alabama's. But Alabama's offense was simple by design.

Coach Bryant would win with what he had. He didn't force a system on a guy. He'd get a guy with heart and desire, and plug him in. And the guy he had at quarterback my freshman year was All-American Pat Trammel. His style wasn't drop back. His style was option. So our offense was option.

You didn't need to be real fancy when the order of the day was to "out-mean" the other side—Coach Bryant's trademark.

I remember standing in practice next to Coach Gene Stallings, then head of the defensive secondary under Coach Bryant, and seeing three players on an adjacent field go into a circle and fight and claw until one went down. A whistle blew, those three guys got out of the way, and three more guys stepped in. I asked Coach Stallings about it.

"Ol' Pat (line Coach Pat James) got him a new drill over there, figured he'd toughen the guys up a bit. Calls it the 'kill or be killed' drill." He laughed.

There was a five foot by four foot sign in our locker room, that read there were five "musts" to play ball at Alabama… YOU MUST BE LEAN, MEAN, MOBILE, AGILE AND HOSTILE. It made me thankful I was a quarterback.

One night a guy walks into my room and points at a girl in a picture I had over my dresser. He asked me if she was my girlfriend. I didn't look up, I just said, "Yeah." I assumed he was pointing at the Homecoming Queen in the picture, who was my girlfriend back home. Later I find out he was pointing at her crown bearer, a black girl. Anyway, pretty soon some guys were calling me nigger lover, Nigger Namath and just plain nigger. These guys just didn't know any better. In Beaver Falls, everyone didn't always get along, but we did live together and work together. Race didn't separate us. In the Jim Crow world, races were separated, so ignorance prevailed.

When you're taught from the moment you are born hatred and intolerance, you believe it's true. To me, I didn't get so angry about being called nigger because it was just so damn stupid. Anyway, I don't know if Coach Bryant heard word about it, but soon the whole thing just died away.

Luckily, I found some kindred spirits at school. We all kind of gravitated to a corner in the union building's cafeteria. We had a big table that sat about twelve – guys from Philadelphia, New Jersey, a couple of track guys from Ithaca, a few from Massachusetts, we'd all hang out in that corner. A couple of northerners who would become close friends were Ray Abruzzese and Jimmy Walsh. Ray was from South Philadelphia. A running back on the varsity by way of Hinds Community College in Mississippi, he took an interest in the kid from the other end of the state, showed me around and gave me the lay of the land. There could be a whole book of Ray Abruzzese stories, but my favorite is this one.

Howard Cosell was talking with Dick Schaap and me one day in our New York apartment. Ray and I shared a place when we both played on the Jets. Howard, Dick and I were in the living room and Howard was, as usual, dominating the conversation. Ray was asleep in his room and I guess Howard's voice woke him up. Ray came into the living room in his loose white T-shirt and silk boxer shorts, rubbing his eyes, and moved toward the TV. He turned and saw Howard and then did a double-take. "Oh, you're *here*," Ray said to Cosell. "I was just coming in to turn you off." Howard was stunned.

My friend Jimmy Walsh is from New Brunswick, New Jersey and we met through Ray. We'd run into each other at Sunday mass or at the pool hall and eventually became good friends, sharing Ray stories and keeping each other out of trouble. We all worked in the summer cutting grass for the maintenance department, working in the paper mill, whatever it took. And our families worked hard too, to help us get through school. Football players would get $15 a month for laundry and I looked for that check every time. My mom would send me a letter with $5 in it every week and I'd wait on that one too. The three of us counted on one another and helped each other out. We were a long way from home.

In June of 1963, I took some summer courses and I had just finished registering. A bunch of us went down to see Alabama Governor George Wallace try and block a young black woman, Vivian Malone, from going to the state's university. The Governor had made a campaign promise a few years before in order to gain office. He got the support of the Ku Klux Klan's Grand Imperial Wizard, Bobby Shelton, by running on a Segregation Forever platform and promised to stand in the schoolhouse door if black people were to be admitted into the university. This is how crazy it was.

I watched from about thirty feet away as the governor began to speak. A federal marshal interrupted him, "Governor Wallace, this is now a federal issue, step aside, please." The governor stepped aside.

by Joe Namath

Shortly thereafter, Vivian Malone registered for classes. I'd see her from time to time and say hello. Most of us at school didn't see what all the fuss was about, and while there were screwballs around (there was a threat and an explosion outside of Vivian's dorm), Vivian completed her schooling.

One of the first, most important lessons I ever learned was from Coach Bryant early during my freshman year. As part of our training, freshman players scrimmaged with the varsity every now and then. Coach Bryant always believed in pressing his players with real contact and competition. Anyway, one afternoon, I was running a run option play. That's a running play where the quarterback takes the ball down the line of scrimmage with a halfback trailing behind him. He has the option of running the ball himself, or pitching it back to the halfback. I got hit, and I dropped it. I fumbled it somehow or made a bad pitch, and I was on the ground, kind of getting up, and Coach Bryant's voice rang out.

"Namath, that is not your job just to go out there..."

Whatever he was yelling about was at me and I knew it was about the pitch, and I'm getting up, and walking back to the huddle. I'm not particularly acknowledging his voice. I just had my head down, kind of nodding. The next thing I knew, he had me by my face mask with his hand and I was on my toes. I mean, he lifted me straight up and looked me in the eye.

"Boy, when I talk to you, you look me in the eye and say, 'Sir!'"

And I'm, "Yes, sir, yes, sir, yes, sir." And by God, I looked him in the eye. He got his point across. If you want to communicate, you'd better learn how it's done. Today, whenever I talk to someone who can't look me in the eye, I wonder just where he's coming from, especially with younger kids. It's like they're in their own little world, not willing to let anyone in. When I was that age, I didn't want to look anyone in the eye either except a teammate, buddy or girlfriend.

From then on, if Coach Bryant ever made a peep that sounded anything like "Joe," I'd hustle right up to him, look him in the eye, and say, "Yes, sir."

Keep in mind, in my freshman year, the Alabama Crimson Tide won every game they played and the National Championship. The quarterback for that

by Joe Namath

squad was Pat Trammell. A freshman quarterback couldn't have had a better guy to try and emulate. Probably the toughest thing to pick up from Pat was his mental-physical toughness. He was tough and mean. A good meanness. I'm talking about a competitive meanness. And the guys really respected Pat. If they didn't, Pat would just fight 'em.

So, why did Coach Bryant take the time to yell at a freshman when he had the best football team in the nation? Coach Bryant did it for everyone on the team. Yeah, the Xs and Os and fundamentals were important, but what made Alabama, Alabama was a coach who cared enough about a kid to teach him how to behave like a man. He taught us how to fight for ourselves, for each other, and for him. But not necessarily in that order.

He used to say that he wanted to coach his players so that they'd be able to face "some morning when you've been out of school twenty years and you wake up and your kids are sick and in bed, your wife is sick and in bed, and you've got the flu just like they have, and you want to stay in bed... You're going to get your butt out of bed and go to work. I'm gonna teach you how to do the kinds of things you'll need to do, even though you don't feel like it." There's not a man who lasted under Coach Bryant who just read this sentence who isn't smiling.

By the time my sophomore year rolled around, Pat Trammell had graduated and left for medical school. Coach Bryant was in need of a new quarterback. He had seven on the roster, and four upperclassmen had the edge. I had a strong showing in spring practice and in the Spring Red-White game, and won the starting job.

I suppose you remember the harsh lessons in your life more than you do your successes. And the lesson that sits in my mind most clearly now from the 1962 season was what happened early in our third game against Vanderbilt. I wasn't playing well and Coach Bryant pulled me out in the middle of a second quarter offensive series. I was coming back to the sidelines and in frustration, I threw my helmet, and sat down on the bench. Coach Bryant walked over to me and sat down too. He looked at me calmly and draped an arm over my shoulder, and it must have looked like he was giving me some nice words of encouragement. In fact, he'd taken a very nice chunk of my neck in his big paw and began squeezing. Quite vigorously.

"Boy, don't ever let me see you act like that again or I'll kick your behind all the way back to Pennsylvania. Don't ever throw your helmet again…or you're gone."

Looking him in the eye I said. "I'm not mad at you, or the coaches, I'm mad at myself for playing so poorly." After a few beats he nodded and left. Maybe it was a lesson for both of us.

by Joe Namath

CHAPTER 04 | Rebel Yell

The Bear Necessities

After Vanderbilt we plowed through Tennessee 35-0, Houston 21-13, and scratched out a battle with Mississippi State. We were winning 20-19, and Coach Bryant put me in the game at left cornerback. Mississippi State, seeing a quarterback on the corner, decided to attack my area. On first down, they tried to beat me deep but I had a good cushion on the receiver and I ended up closest to the overthrown ball. On second down, they came out on a sweep to my side with two big ol' linemen leading the way for a huge fullback name Hoyle Grange. Hoyle was an agile load and would go on to play pro ball.

The linemen both peeled back to block and left me one-on-one with the ball carrier. I was able to cut him down for a yard loss. It felt just wonderful. Third down, they came with a roll-out pass away from me, and remembering our scouting report and having good football instinct, I started yelling, "Throw back, Charlie, throw back!" And the quarterback pulls up, turns around, and throws it right back to our linebacker Charlie Stephens, who intercepts it, and we win 20-19. The coaches gave me a game ball. Still have that one.

We were streaking toward the National Championship at 8-0 when we went down at Georgia Tech's Grant Field. The pre-game hype reached almost riot-like proportions. There was still serious bad blood between the Tide and the Yellow Jackets from two seasons earlier. A diminutive linebacker (diminutive like the Tasmanian Devil) from Alabama named Darwin Holt accidentally broke the jaw of a Georgia Tech player named Chick Graning. It was an outrageous hit certainly, since it appeared to be intentional. I mean, Graning was looking up at the football, catching a punt, and the timing of Holt was perfect. The ball came into him, just as Holt left his feet, leading with the forearm, and hit him. There has been much debate about whether or not it was a clean shot—if Graning had signaled a fair catch or not before Holt hit him. Now, as a guy who has been hit dirty and clean, I can sympathize with the outrage of the Tech team and fans, but films show that Holt never saw the fair catch signal before he hit Graning.

Anyway, the press went wild and accused Coach Bryant of fielding a team of hellions. Furman Bisher of the *Atlanta Journal-Constitution* was the leading voice in the charge. We were in for a battle. The fans pelted us with all kinds of garbage on the sidelines—Coach Bryant took a hit from an airborne Jack Daniels bottle.

In the fourth quarter, down 7-0, our punt-return team came through and blocked a Tech punt. We were able to take it in after that and close the score to 7-6. Coach Bryant went for the two-point conversion instead of the single point tie. We didn't make it.

We lost and it cost us the National Championship.

But that wasn't the end of the season. After the Tech game, we beat Auburn 38-0 then Bud Wilkinson's Oklahoma Sooners 17-0 in front of President John F. Kennedy at the Miami Orange Bowl on New Year's Day, 1963.

The following semester, I was invited to join the "A Club," the university's fraternity for varsity lettermen. My buddy Ray Abruzzese had no real interest in having his head shaved, drinking Tabasco juice, and having his rear end tattooed with a paddle just so he could wear a cardigan sweater around campus with an "A" on it. And neither did I.

Now, I had had my butt paddled before. In junior high school, it was normal for kids with a disciplinary problem to get hit with an inch-and-a-half-by-three-foot paddle (I guess you could call it a flat club), especially in metal shop. Our shop teacher would have you bend over and hold onto your ankles, and he'd give you a whack with that board if you ever misbehaved. I'd been through it and I didn't want anybody doing that to me again. And why? To join a club? I had *earned* my letter!

One afternoon, Coach Bryant called me to his office. Now this wasn't exactly a daily occurrence. It was sort of like being in class and having the principal coming to pull you out. You know right then that something is dirty in the milk. He's either going to punish you or expel you.

"Come on, let's take a ride." I tell you, from the office to the car was a long walk in silence.

Finally in the car, he got right to the point, "I understand you're not going through A Club initiation."

"Yes, sir, that's right."

"Why not?"

"I don't believe in it. I don't believe in shaving my head and getting hit with a paddle. I earned my letter and I think I should be able to wear it without going through that stuff."

He understood that because he knew me. We'd been together for a while now, and that's just the way that I felt.

"Well, you know Joe; going through A club is a tradition here."

And I said, "Yes, sir, that's fine."

And then he said, "You know, you can't be a captain unless you're in the A Club."

And I said, "Well, sir, that's all right."

And then he was quiet for a while and said with his beautifully commanding voice, "Well, I want you to!"

"Yes, sir."

And that was that.

I wouldn't say no to Coach Bryant. I guess I could have, but at that point, I wouldn't.

Because I missed the first meeting for our new A Club inductees, I paid for it. The guys gave me a pretty rough time. There were 27 initiates that year—we called ourselves the Magnificent 27. We looked anything but magnificent with our heads shaved and wearing only coveralls and sneakers.

The A Club thing with Coach Bryant kind of stuck in my craw. But I did learn to understand why he asked me to go through with it. He wanted me to be one of the guys.

Around the same time, coach Bryant brought in Coach Kenny Meyer, for his expertise of the passing game, to complement the rest of our offense. Coach Bryant decided to mix in a drop back passing game with two wide receivers and we began the year with big wins over Georgia, Tulane, and Vanderbilt, outscoring the opposition 81-13. When Florida came to Tuscaloosa, we were supposed to win. When anybody came to Tuscaloosa, we were supposed to win. Coach Bryant had never had a team lose in Denny Stadium. But someone forgot to tell the Gators. They stopped us at the goal line twice and I threw two interceptions. We lost 10-6. Coach Bryant said, "We plumb gave out."

I remember the game alright—so much so that I don't really want to relive it. They were good. And we didn't play well. When Coach Bryant said that we gave out, I hate to think about that even now, because that meant the following week we had some awful tough practices. When he said we *plumb gave out*, it meant that he and his staff didn't have us in good enough condition with the proper attitude.

Coach Bryant found a way to get us refocused, and we followed our loss to Florida with wins over Tennessee, Houston, and Mississippi State.

Now we were hosting a home game with Georgia Tech, and we had a payback attitude. As I'd played poorly over at Tech before, I tried to redeem myself. Having thrown more than usual for an Alabama offense in our first seven games, we suspected the Rambling Wreck had prepared itself for a passing attack. So, we zigged instead of zagged. We only threw the ball four times. My roommate, Tight End Pelham Butch Henry, caught one of them for 11 yards. Two fell incomplete, and one was flagged for interference, which set up our last touchdown. I ran instead (eleven times for 53 yards) and we ground out a 27-11 win.

Now anytime you hold a team at 11 points, you're supposed to win. Whatever way our offense scored, it was our defense that did a heck of a job. We played Alabama football, Coach Bryant football through and through— tough and mean. Our next game would be against the Auburn Tigers.

Early in the week I was in the dorm in my bunk catching a nap, and my teammate from Youngstown, Ohio, Frank Cicatiello woke me up with the news: President Kennedy was assassinated. We were both stunned, of course. First place we went was over to church and after that, it was like all of us, the whole country, had had the wind knocked out of us, gasping, not believing. Your mind couldn't help but be on what just took place.

We didn't lose the game over that, certainly. We lost the game because I played like a mutt, and you know what? If your defense holds a team to 11 points, they did more than their job. We didn't score enough, and that falls on the quarterback. I stunk, I still don't like the memory. We lost 11-8.

Now's about the time I should tell you about my good buddy, Jack Horace "Hoot Owl" Hicks. He never liked anyone knowing his middle name, Horace. I can't blame him. Jack grew up about thirty miles from Tuscaloosa in a place called West Blocton and he knew his way around. On scholarship as one of the team's managers, Jack looked just like this cartoon character Ollie Owl, so the guys ended up calling him "Hoot Owl." One of the first times I met him was when I was issued my number. You don't get to choose your number as a football player until you've earned the right. As a freshman, I had no rights. I expected none anyway.

When I did have it handed to me, it was #12. Now, #12 was Pat Trammell's number on the varsity. Coach Bryant thought the world of Pat, and maybe he had something to do with my receiving it. It certainly inspired me to live up to that honor. Some reporter once asked Coach Bryant about Pat's skills: "As a quarterback, Pat has no ability...all he can do is beat you," he said. In my senior year at Alabama, another freshman quarterback received #12. His name was Kenny "the Snake" Stabler.

Hoot Owl and I pooled what money we could get together and bought a '54, four-door Ford. We took the doors off. It wasn't illegal at the time, and no one said anything. No big deal, just a couple of college kids riding around in this car with no doors. I mean people ride in open Jeeps, don't they? But we were very careful about not making fools of ourselves or doing anything that would compromise our training. Coach Bryant had strict rules against drinking. Drinking and smoking was against all Coach's rules back then. The smoking ban was certainly a double standard because the coaches lit up in the locker rooms, in meetings, and on the fields so much that we were practically smoking anyway. But rules were rules, and we tried to follow them.

We weren't supposed to, but some of us had a beer or two after a game or on a Saturday night. But during the week, we had curfew, man. We had to be in. Even if you were a senior, you still had to be in by 11 p.m. One night Hoot Owl and I were out with a bunch of guys and there was some drinking going on. I didn't have much, just enough.

On Monday morning in the cafeteria, Coach Bryant said he wanted to talk to me and I followed him back to one of the guestrooms in the dorm. I got a case of bad butterflies, I knew something was up and I sure didn't feel comfortable about it.

"Joe, somebody got in touch with me and said you were acting up Saturday afternoon. He said you'd been drinking and you were out directing traffic. I believe this gentleman for his word, but I'll take your word first 'cause I know you wouldn't lie to me," he said.

"No, sir," I said. "That's a lie. I wasn't drunk and I wasn't directing traffic downtown Saturday afternoon."

"You didn't drink at all Saturday?" Now why did he have to go and ask that? "Yes sir, I did."

Well, what happened right then was he fell down, I mean, he was standing up talking to me and when I gave him the answer, he fell backwards onto the bed. I thought he had a heart attack.

He just fell back on the bed and said, "Ohhh." He started rolling back and forth and moaning. I asked him if he was okay. He just moaned a few more times and then he got up and he said, "Well, I'm gonna have to suspend you. Come over to the coaches' office after—I have a meeting with the coaches— come over at two o'clock."

Coach Bryant met me in the reception area of the office, and there were other coaches mingling about. We stood there and he said, "Well, we had our meeting, and a lot of coaches think we should be able to discipline you in some other way than to suspend you." And he said, "I'd go along with my coaches, but if I do that, it's going against what I believe in—I let you play, I'll retire."

Now, I wasn't stupid enough to think that he actually meant those words that way. But he did let me know that he didn't agree with his other coaches. I was embarrassed and, I remember exactly what I said. "I don't want you to do that, Coach." Like I thought he really would. I was a 19-year-old kid, you know, so embarrassed for letting him down.

 He kept right on, "Well, we're gonna put you in another dorm." He just went rolling right along, and he found me another place to live. I had to move out of Paul W. Bryant Hall and move over to Paty Hall, a regular student dorm. I wasn't allowed to hang with the team, and I had to watch the last two games against Miami and our Sugar Bowl appearance as a spectator. I thanked my team and my God that we won.

Being suspended hurt real bad. Coach Bryant called my mother and told her what had happened. He also let her know that I would have the opportunity to rejoin the team if I earned my way back. Mom could deal with that. He probably had something to do with alerting another lady who really helped me. Mrs. Mary Harmon Bryant called and invited me over for dinner and strengthened my determination to stay in school with mother-like affection. She also made sure I didn't do something stupid like play Canadian football or hitchhike to Wrigley Field, things I actually considered soon after it happened.

While I was suspended, Steve Sloan, the best college quarterback I'd seen up to that time, took my place. I thought he was brilliant. The following season in '65, the Tide won the National Championship with him. I mean, Steve could play. Now, if your team loses when you don't play, you feel like you really let them down, more so than if they win. And to break a rule and get kicked off the team and then have your team go and lose would have really stunk. I was lucky. Coach Bryant reinforced another life lesson—no one player is bigger than the team.

I moved into Paty Hall. I felt lost and out of place and for the second time in my life, I was not part of the team. It brought back some of the painful memories of not being invited to my old high school football camp. I didn't belong. I didn't measure up. I didn't deserve to be on the team.

In Alabama, the interest spread about why I was suspended. There were nasty stories circulating about me and it was tough. Not only did I feel lost, I was very self-conscious about people talking about me in a negative way. I'd see somebody looking at me and I'd rattle things around in my mind about how lousy they thought I was. It felt awful.

I had to own up. There was a probationary period until 1964's spring practice. During that period, I behaved myself, trained hard and when I came out for practice, Coach Bryant had me on the fifth string. By the end of the spring practices, I'd earned my way back to the first string. Physically I felt great at 6' 2", a lean 195 lbs., and had worked on my footwork and agility throughout the winter. I wanted to play!

The first two games of the season I carried the ball 22 times, averaged 4.8 yards a carry, and led the nation in scoring, running for five touchdowns. I'd been clocked in the 40-yard dash at 4.7 seconds in full pads (without helmet). This was the college quarterback era of Fran Tarkenton at Georgia and Roger "the Dodger" Staubach at Navy, scramblers who played a ball-control kind of game. College quarterbacks were expected to make things happen with their minds first, their feet second, and their arms third.

After three games, I felt strong in every part of my skills set. Coach Bryant gave his quarterbacks control of the play calling. But we had to convince him and Coach Kutchens, our quarterback coach, that the plays we called when facing a specific defensive alignment made sense in given down and distance situations. Some of us called better plays than others. And I think play calling was a forte of mine. My feet and legs felt light, moving effortlessly, already knowing with good anticipation of when to cut and juke. And my arm was pretty good too, but with our running game performing the way it was, we didn't need to use it all that often.

North Carolina State came to Tuscaloosa undefeated. They had a good team, and they had Tony Golmont playing defensive back for them, a buddy that I had played ball with in Beaver Falls. So, a bunch of guys from Beaver Falls drove down to Tuscaloosa—relatives, friends of ours, a whole crew. The night before the game, the Beaver Falls guys were allowed to visit me out at the Moon Winks Hotel, where Coach Bryant put us up the night before a home game.

Of course, the guys from home were looking for some kind of edge. One said, "Holy Cow, Joe, you know North Carolina State's undefeated, man." I said, "Yeah, I know." He said, "You know, you guys are 20-point favorites." And I'm real careful here because you can't talk about points and gambling in any way, shape, or form.

So I said, "Is that right?"

He said, "You think you—"

I cut him off and said, "That sounds like a lot, but I do know one thing. I wouldn't bet against us." We won 21-0.

We couldn't have had a better day to play. It was sunny, about 70 degrees, clear, windless, and we were still undefeated. Before the game in the locker room, I was so excited I forgot to tape my shoes, something I did for luck, support, and style. I also put my thigh pads in backwards. For some reason, I had an awful clumsy time getting ready for that game.

We were hot in the first quarter, completing seven of eight passes, but it was still scoreless. On the first play of the second quarter, we were in a third down and one situation. To this day, I believe a run pass option is the best play in football, if you have somebody who can do it consistently. I called it. I rolled out to my right, looking to grab that yard for the first down, and if it wasn't there, then a receiver had to be open. I cut back to the left inside and I must have hit a bad spot on the field because my right knee just snapped. The movement of it—I felt the thing kind of cave inward.

It was so sudden; it reminds me of when I hear people describe being shot. I was never shot; I don't know what that's like. But it was going from one instant you're fine and the next you're engulfed in pain. They didn't tell me much; our trainer Jim Goostree, examined my leg, and as I'm lying there looking at him, he didn't look real positive. He held my leg up in the air and held the bottom of my foot to evaluate the knee's stability. I guess there wasn't the kind of stability he was looking for, so he knew something was wrong.

I was able to walk off the field, and we just put ice on it, and I stood the rest of the game as a cheerleader, watching the game, knowing something was wrong with my knee but not exactly what. At the hospital after the game, we found out something was, in fact, torn. Because when we drained it—aspirated

it—the fluid was bloody. But we didn't know what was torn. We didn't have today's arthroscopic technology to look inside and see what was wrong. They did do what they call an arthrogram, where they inject air and dye into the joint, and when the dye settles, you can sometimes tell what's torn. But the bottom line was, I wanted to play, and I was given that opportunity.

I was just getting started in my life and football was what I was good at. I believed that I needed to play with pain, not because I liked it, of course, but because I believed I needed to play. I convinced myself that playing football was the best way for me to continue to grow. Now, if it were just impossible for me to play physically, I would have become a school teacher and a coach. But I didn't want to own up to that possibility—that I was finished. I convinced

myself I needed to play or I'd be doing something else that I didn't love nearly as much as playing football. You see, there was something ingrained in me telling me that I could still play. I just couldn't do it the way that I'd like to do it or would certainly have preferred to do it. So I made compensations, learned my limitations. I knew what not to do. If I thought about sprinting right, a bell inside my brain would go off and say, "Whoa, easy boy."

My knee was a focus breaker at practice, for sure—every time I practiced pain was involved. And sometimes it got to the point where the swelling might not allow me to be on my feet as much, but as long as the swelling wasn't there, I could be out there practicing. And yeah, it hurt, but it wasn't debilitating. I accepted it.

Sometimes I would imagine myself playing with healthy wheels, but I knew it was a waste of time. My whole life, up to this point, I was quick, fast and used my gifts athletically. Now, I was an athlete who couldn't run very well.

You know what I did figure out? If I hadn't hurt my knee, I'd have probably ended up in Vietnam, been wounded or killed like so many of our fathers, mothers and sons were. I look at this knee injury as a blessing in disguise. I believe things could have always been worse and I considered myself lucky.

Coach Bryant used me sparingly, and it was a cycle of play, buckle, swell, ice, needle, play, buckle, swell, ice, needle, play… He said of me, "He moves like a human now. He did move like a cat."

We made it to 8-0 with Steve Sloan carrying the load and with me coming in off the bench now and again to toss a few downfield. Two games stood between us and an undefeated season: against our old friends the Rambling Wrecks of Georgia Tech and our intrastate rival the Auburn War Eagles.

The day before the game we were leaving Tuscaloosa to go to Atlanta and play Tech. When we got on the plane, Coach Bryant told me, "Sit down, Joe."

I was sitting beside him and I was a senior, and he shared with me that this was the last time we were going to play Georgia Tech. The relationship between the two teams' athletic departments had become so hostile that Coach Bryant decided not to renew the schedule.

When we arrived at Grant Field in Atlanta, we headed straight to the locker room. It felt like very serious business as usual. We were pretty quiet—before a game with Coach Bryant, your mind was supposed to be on the game, so you didn't giggle and carry on. You could talk to one another, but with low voices. Keep a low profile. Prior to each game we'd take a walk around the playing field to get a feel for the place. So, dressed in our crimson blazers Coach Bryant starts leading us out there, and he's carrying a helmet. We're walking along and with that wonderful grin of his, he puts on the helmet and looks up at the Georgia Tech fans and says, "Yeah y'all go ahead and throw your whiskey bottles now." The few of us that heard this passed Coach's fighting words back through the line, and I could feel the energy change. We walked around the field behind him, as ready for a game as we'd ever been.

Those students were crazy, they would throw all kinds of crap, and man, it was wild. And he had that helmet on and it loosened us up.

The game was dead even, but we'd just recovered a Tech fumble at their 49. I threw an out pattern that the DB almost picked off. Then we came right back with an out and up deep to David Ray. He caught it for a 48-yard gain. Steve Bowman scored on the next play. We kicked the extra point, and were up 7-0 with under a minute left in the half.

Coach Bryant, who till this day has the reputation of being a conservative coach, went for the on-sides kick and we recovered. I called an out and up and in. Heck, why not? Ray Ogden caught it for 45 yards, and then I hit David Ray for a touchdown. In 78 seconds, we scored 14 points. Coach gave me the rest of the game off.

After Georgia Tech, we had to beat Auburn to go undefeated. The year before, we had lost 11-8 to these guys. Also, Auburn had a Heisman trophy candidate, Tucker Frederickson. We played on Thanksgiving Day at Legion Field in front of a sell-out house. Down 7-6, I came in late in the second quarter and threw deep. It was picked off and we went in at halftime with some things to think about. In the second half, Steve Sloan hurt his knee and I finished out the game. The capper was a 22-yard strike to Ray Perkins which sealed the deal for us and the National Championship with a 21-14 win.

After the game I was helping Steve Sloane get his sock on. He was hurting and couldn't bend his knee so well. Coach Bryant came over, getting a little kick out of the sight, and said, "Oh, by the way, you know these pro scouts are gonna be coming around talking to you now."

"Yes, sir," I said.

"Do you have any idea what you're gonna ask for?"

I said, "Well, Coach, last year Don Trull (Baylor's QB) got $100,000 or so, so I figured I'd go ahead and ask them for something around there."

And Coach Bryant was just quiet for a few beats and said, "You go ahead and ask them for $200,000. That's a better place to start."

Coach Bryant told this story in his autobiography.

I'll never forget the last game of Joe's senior year, in the dressing room after we'd beaten Auburn. We were the only two still in there. And he said something that made me about as proud as I've ever been.

He said, "I want to look you in the eye"— that's one of my pet expressions— "I want to look you right in the eye and tell you, you were right, and I want to thank you."

I wouldn't take a jillion for that.

That's another lesson Coach Bryant taught me. You don't just tell people what's wrong with them; you thank them when they do something right. He

did something right when he suspended me. It helped me appreciate the game and its people more and to walk a straighter line to continue playing. Being a part of a team is a privilege, not a right. He made me a better person.

We'd play Texas in the Orange Bowl on New Year's Day to cap off our year. Even though we were declared the National Champions by the Associated Press poll, we were underdogs going into the game. My knee was still a major uncertainty and Steve Sloan's knee injury in the Auburn game didn't help either.

Texas was coached by Darrell Royal, a friend of Coach Bryant's who played quarterback for Oklahoma Coach Bud Wilkinson and was instrumental in the development of the wishbone offense. Coach Bryant had never defeated a Coach Royal team, but through the years had exchanged ideas with Royal and even recommended him to the University of Texas for the head coaching job when it became available in 1956. The only three television networks in existence were in the middle of a ratings fight and NBC decided that it was the perfect time to debut primetime football, not just primetime college football, but *primetime* football.

The January 1, 1965 Alabama-Texas Orange Bowl was also the first sporting event broadcast in color and would draw a record audience of some 25 million people. And after shelling out $600,000 to the Orange Bowl Committee for the rights, NBC introduced a new technology called "instant replay." Advertising agencies were licking their chops because there were companies lined up, wanting to reach the male audience. What better way than to advertise during a football game at night?

So what happens? Six days before the game, I hurt my knee again—unloading the trunk of the car. I didn't practice much. I didn't think I was a part of the plan.

New Year's Day evening, I hobbled on to the Orange Bowl field in soccer shoes, to avoid cleats catching in the turf. Just prior to the National Anthem, I was standing between Coach Bryant and head trainer Jim Goostree. I hadn't practiced for the last six days because of my knee, and I really didn't think I would play.

Coach Bryant said, "Jim, can he play?" I looked at Coach Goostree, and he looked at me and answered, "I think so, Coach." Wake up call.

The Longhorns hit us hard and often in the first quarter. Ernie Koy, their star running back, goes 79 yards for a touchdown. Then, on their next possession, Texas quarterback Jim Hudson hits George Sauer, Jr. for a 69-yard touchdown pass. We're down 14-0, and it's only the beginning of the second quarter. Steve Sloan's knee is killing him. Coach Bryant sends me in.

I called every play from that point forward, and we fought and scrapped as hard as we could. We drove down the field and scored. 14-7. Texas recovered an Alabama punt block punt for a first down and closed out the half with another touchdown. Texas 21, Alabama 7 at the half.

We came out and scored quickly in the third quarter. Wide receiver Ray Perkins made a heck of a catch for a 20-yard touchdown pass and now we're back in the game, 21-14. We held them. We drove back down to their 8. The drive stalled. We kicked a field goal, making it 21-17, with most of the fourth quarter to go.

We intercepted a Texas pass. A few throws of our own got us down to their 6-yard line. We ran the ball three times and got within one foot of the goal line. If I had everything to do over again, I'd have called time out after first down and gone over there and talked to Coach Bryant. Or after second down. I shoulda, shoulda, shoulda… Going into fourth down there, the best play to run would've been the run pass option. And I couldn't do that because of my leg.

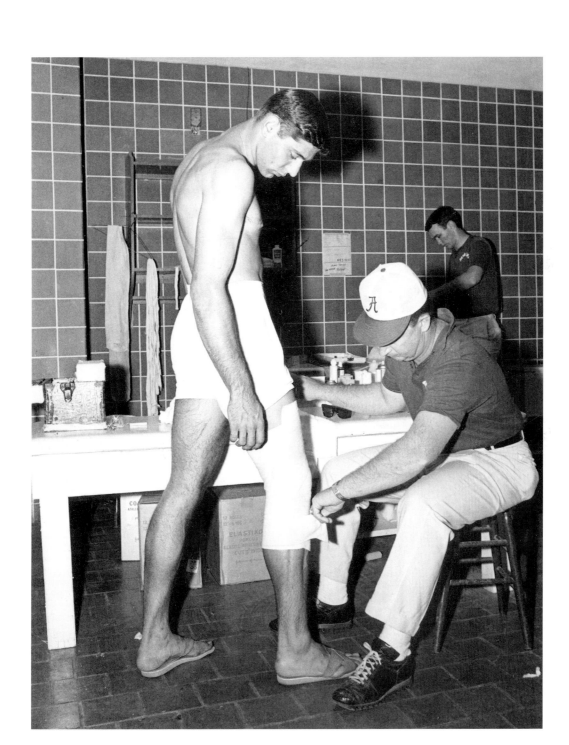

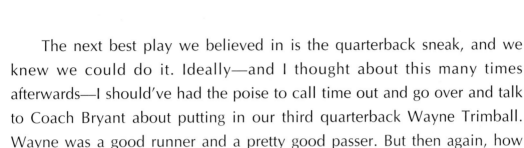
The next best play we believed in is the quarterback sneak, and we knew we could do it. Ideally—and I thought about this many times afterwards—I should've had the poise to call time out and go over and talk to Coach Bryant about putting in our third quarterback Wayne Trimball. Wayne was a good runner and a pretty good passer. But then again, how would the ten guys out there on the field feel about a substitution at this point? Catch-22.

I called a quarterback sneak, got hit by Texas linebacker/tight end Pete Lammons. Laying in the pile, looking across the field to the linesman I saw the touchdown signal.

Then there was a conference between all of the officials, and the linesman who signaled the score backed down. Just like that, I was over the goal line but did not score a touchdown. No touchdown. We lost the game.

I was named Most Valuable Player of the Orange Bowl, but MVP is little consolation after a loss. I forgot to pick up the trophy. The next day I went to the Bal Harbour Inn and signed the largest contract ever negotiated to play professional football. The New York Jets' president and part owner, Mr. David A. Werblin, and Head Coach Weeb Ewbank made sure I put pen to paper.

Looking back now, I understand why Coach Bryant took me on that drive and asked me to join the A Club. And I joined a club because a man I respected asked me to. In return, I had guys on my team play their hearts out in front of me, who were outweighed by at least 20 to 30 lbs. per man. They held off

Texas blitzes that would have eaten up any other line in the country. And I had the trust of the greatest football coach in the world. When I called the quarterback sneak that became the touchdown that wasn't, Coach Bryant told the press he made that call. I wouldn't take a jillion for that myself.

CHAPTER 05 | It's Hard to Be a Saint in the City

Rookie Year

The first time I walked into our locker room at Shea Stadium I was with Head Coach Weeb Ewbank and a bunch of guys from the media. We were going to test my newly repaired right knee going through some drills on the field.

When we returned to the locker room our revered equipment manger, Bill Hampton asked me if I wanted to meet Don Maynard, the Jets' starting receiver, and I said, "Yeah, sure." He took me over and introduced me to Maynard, this lean 6' 3" Texan. Don put his arm around me, turned me aside, and said, "Hey listen here, son. All these guys here, they're shaking your hand, and they're patting you on the back now. They're all smiling and saying things are good, and that's great. But in this game, there comes a time when they may not even say goodbye to you. Just go. They're finished with you. So remember: This is a business. It's a cold-blooded business." He was doing me a favor, and I didn't even know it.

Don didn't talk about the upcoming season or how we'd do this, that or the other. That veteran tall Texan just saw everybody there catering to a 21-year-old kid who hadn't even been in a pro locker room before, and he set me straight.

Now one of the first things they did to rookies was measure their heads. But for me, considering the fact that the New York Jets had placed almost half the franchise money on my wobbly right knee, they didn't pull out the tape measure until training camp. Instead, being the PR genius that he was, Mr. Werblin threw a party for the media. The place? Toots Shor's.

Now on January 22, 1965, Giant great Y.A. Tittle retired at Mama Leone's at lunchtime. Mamma Leone's was the old blueblood Giant kind of place. I always heard about it, and when I finally went, all I saw was blue. All I felt was

that blue. So, Mr. Werblin brought that same crowd across town for a Jet cocktail party. I was the appetizer, entrée, and dessert all rolled into one for New York's mischievous media—its sportswriters, three television reporters, radio guys, and general sporting crowd.

Toots Shor was the kind of guy who thought dumping a scotch in your lap was high comedy and lukewarm roumaki (liver with bacon wrapped around it) was five-star cuisine. And his joint was old school. This was the home of the New York Giants' Frank Gifford, the New York Yankees' Joe DiMaggio, TV's Jackie Gleason, and even the Catholic Church's Cardinal Spellman. And in 1965, the New York Jets were no school, a joke. We got no respect from these people.

You see, the Jets didn't even play in the NFL! They were part of a maverick set of teams called the American Football League, started up when I was a junior in high school by a 26-year-old Texan named Mr. Lamar Hunt. At first, Mr. Hunt went to the NFL owners and politely suggested that their game could be much bigger if they added franchises in new cities. They froze him out. So he did what a lot of young people with desire and financial wherewithal do. He started his own thing. The AFL began with eight teams in New York, Los Angeles (it would move to San Diego), Oakland, Houston, Boston, Dallas (it would move to Kansas City), Denver, and Buffalo.

Mr. Hunt believed that professional football could become an even bigger American phenomenon than Major League Baseball. But it needed more franchises in more cities. There were only 432 players in the entire NFL, 36 guys on each of the twelve teams, three of which were on the taxi (players who practice, but aren't on the game-day roster). And with so many outstanding college players to choose from and so many innovative coaches across the country, there was obviously more than enough talent to form another league.

AFL Founders (left to right): Bud Adams, Harry Wismer, Lamar Hunt, Robert Howsam, and Sydney Latham

But stadium seats weren't exactly filled in the NFL. How did Mr. Hunt expect to fill them up in a new league? Television. Baseball was okay television, but football was great television! Johnny U. and the Colts proved that in 1958. And the networks, NBC, CBS, and ABC, loved that advertisers wanted to reach people who liked to watch football games. So, Mr. Hunt and his "foolish club" of rich owners went in and sold ABC the TV rights for $8,925,000 dollars (about $1.08 billion in today's dollars)—before the AFL even played one game!

Then, they started going after talent. The AFL had their own college draft and with the TV money, battled their competition. My freshman year at Alabama, the 1959 Heisman trophy winner, Billy Cannon, was the #1 draft pick of the Los Angeles Rams of the NFL. The Rams general manager, a young lawyer named Pete Rozelle, signed Cannon to a contract that gave him a $10,000 signing bonus, and salaries of $15,000 a year for three years, plus he threw in $500 to cover travel expenses. That deal was the best contract for a professional football player at the time. In today's money, this would be equal to about a $125,000 signing bonus, plus an annual salary of $189,000 and $6,300 of travel expenses. A nice living for sure, but compare Cannon's deal to what a recent #1 draft pick, Mario Williams, received from the Houston Texans—a 24 million dollar guaranteed signing bonus, plus $5 million dollars a year in salary for six years.

There was one semi-major detail that Billy needed to clear up. And that was that he signed his NFL contract before the end of his college eligibility, which was strictly forbidden by the NCAA and the NFL. If the truth of Cannon's signing had come out before he played in the 1959 Sugar Bowl, he would have been disciplined by the NCAA and declared ineligible for the game.

Because Cannon wasn't returning their phone calls, the AFL team that held his rights, the Houston Oilers, suspected that he had secretly signed with the NFL. So, they doubled the Rams offer and made sure that he signed his

Oiler contract the second he finished playing the Sugar Bowl. The press witnessed the signing and made it terribly embarrassing for the NFL's Rams to reveal that Cannon was already under contract, which was against college and NFL rules. But the Rams did it anyway.

Now, the only way that Cannon's team (LSU) could keep its win in that year's Sugar Bowl and its 11-0 record was for the NFL contract to be annulled. So after the lawyers were through, the Oilers got Cannon, and LSU kept its National Championship. The Cannon incident brought the NFL and the AFL to war.

This was really good for guys like me. Prices for players went up, and since I was playing some pretty good football for a coach named Paul "Bear" Bryant (an ace in the hole for any prospective pro player) and 1964's #1 college football team, the NFL and AFL took some serious interest in me. They began their bidding even before the season ended.

The New York Giants controlled the first pick of the NFL draft. Since their quarterback, Y.A. Tittle, was close to retirement, many football writers thought there was a good chance they'd pick me. The Houston Oilers and Head Coach Slingin' Sammy Baugh controlled the rights to the first pick of the AFL. Their scouting report on me was the best report card I've ever had.

The New York Giants selected Auburn running back Tucker Frederickson as the NFL's #1 and then the Houston Oilers selected Baylor tight end Lawrence Elkins as the AFL's #1. Eventually I was picked in the NFL's first round by the St. Louis Cardinals, #12 overall, and in the AFL's first round, #5 overall, by the New York Jets.

The thing of it was, though, in 1964, the pro football draft was not even close to what it is today. There was very little attention paid to the selections, and with no ESPN soundstages, podiums, or photo ops, college players were in the dark, to a large extent, about what team drafted whom, when or why.

You didn't know much. You weren't aware of the details. And sports agents were not the factor they are today.

I didn't have many hopes in landing a big contract, anyway. I was pessimistic and afraid to think that I'd go high. I had a bad knee. And it hurt. *What* people in their right mind would go ahead and take a guy in a high round with a bum knee? So maybe I was playing a mind game with myself and trying to ignore the draft.

I just knew where I was, man, and my knee was bad. And you know what, Coach Bryant might have suspected my state of mind (he knew me better than I knew myself at this point in my life), so he gave me some advice that set me straight.

One of the owners and the general manager from the Cardinals came unannounced to my dorm. I had to go downstairs to the foyer to sign them in. We went upstairs to my room and they both sat down on my bunk and I sat on my roommate's bunk.

Although I wasn't a great judge of personalities then, I wasn't totally comfortable with the way that they carried themselves. We got the introductions out the way and bup, bup, bup, "We want to sign you. What would it take to sign you?" I was totally embarrassed and all. It was just me and those two guys in my room, right? And I said, "Uh, yeah, $200,000." Now they're both sitting there in what appeared to be a state of shock, and one of them goes, "Oh $200,000!"

But I wasn't finished. I had to be brave. "And a new car," I said.

"New car, huh? Oh, well… What kind of car?"

"A Lincoln Continental convertible."

"Well sure, who wouldn't?"

Well, they sounded so put off about what I asked for it surprised me that they turned around and immediately agreed. They produced a contract and wanted to me to sign with them, right then and there. I don't blame them. But I said, "No, I have to get a lawyer. I'm not signing anything till after the Orange Bowl, and I need to talk to the NY Jets before I commit to anyone." My mother was still sending me $5 a week in the mail. You know what I'm saying? I had the good sense to call a lawyer friend of mine, Mike Bite of Bite, Bite & Bite of Birmingham. I put the negotiations in Mike's hands.

Now, the New York Jets had risen from the ashes of a franchise called the New York Titans, a team founded by one of the best promoters since P.T. Barnum. Harry Wisner, best known as a radio commentator for the Washington Redskins and Notre Dame, had somehow put together enough of a stake to buy into Mr. Lamar Hunt's AFL.

The New York Titans played in the cavernous Polo Grounds and fielded some very good football players. Don Maynard, Larry Grantham, Curley Johnson and Billy Mathis were original Titans who ended up playing on the Jets. Maynard, though drafted by the Giants, was cut because he wasn't really a Giant kind of player. Don, a true original, wore long sideburns, cowboy boots, and talked with a thick West Texas twang. Fast as lightning with incredible hands, it's no wonder he went in to the Hall of Fame. But to the Giants, who didn't throw the ball downfield all that much, Don was disposable.

Unfortunately, Mr. Wisner just didn't have the know-how or the deep pockets to get people in the seats. And at the end of the 1962 season, with the Titans' checks bouncing like ping pong balls and Wisner facing bankruptcy, the AFL's anchor TV franchise was in serious trouble. In stepped David A. "Sonny" Werblin and his partners, Leon Hess, Phil Iselin, Donald Lillis, and Townsend Martin, who formed the Gotham Football Club, Inc. They bought the Titans for $1,000,000 and renamed them the Jets to rhyme with New York's new baseball team, the Mets. Mr. Werblin, the former head of the Music Corporation of America (MCA), knew his way around show business. While

Don Maynard

Larry Grantham

Bill Mathis

Curley Johnson

he didn't pretend to know much about the Xs and Os of the game, Mr. Werblin understood what entertained people—stars and stories. He believed in the star system, filling the stands by promoting individual men on the field that the average Joe could relate to or aspire to be.

And he decided that football could be chockfull of stars and stories. He and his Jets would take the message wide. The Jets—each individual Jet player— were the future. Before I came to New York, the Jets had lost over $1.4 million in two years, but it didn't worry Mr. Werblin. Despite the losses, he was close to capacity at Shea Stadium every Sunday. He felt that he was one player away from turning the Jets into a money-maker.

The first time I met Mr. Werblin was in a hotel in Birmingham, Alabama. I was impressed by his demeanor, his sincerity and his manners. He also made me believe in the AFL and the New York Jets.

Before the Orange Bowl, Mike reported in to me as St. Louis and the Jets kept in close contact. Mr. Werblin kept in touch personally and then he invited Mike and me out to a Jets game in San Diego. We paid our own way because Coach Bryant was insistent that I didn't accept anything from them before our Bowl game. "I don't even want you to take a Coca-Cola."

Mr. Werblin used that line for PR: "The AFL is straight. This negotiation is straight. They won't even let me buy the kid a Coca-Cola. We don't break rules like the NFL did with Billy Cannon."

What I was really looking forward to about Mr. Werblin's invitation is that he got us rooms at the Beverly Hills Hotel before we went to San Diego. I marveled at the wallpaper. It was like walking through a jungle with all the leaves, flowers and colors. For a night or two we did the negotiations and laid out the groundwork for the contract.

When he began, Mr. Werblin said, "Look, we're not going to get into a bidding war over you. We're going to give you more than they will." He began at three hundred grand, a hundred more than we had even asked for with the Cardinals. We were kind of caught off guard there. Mike and I went into the next room worked out a few details and when we came back, we agreed in principal that I wanted to work with the New York Jets. And then we went down to San Diego.

When we got to San Diego, I saw Chuck Knox, the Coach from Ellwood City, Pennsylvania who befriended me in ninth grade. He was now the Jets offensive line coach and also one of their top college scouts. I'd later learn that he reported on me:

An outstanding passer, with big, good hands and exceptionally fast delivery. Has good agility and sets-up very well—a fine 'scrambler.' Throws the short pass very well and can also throw the 'bomb' with great accuracy. Is smart and follows the 'game plan' perfectly. Is a fine Leader and the Team has great confidence in him. Will be everyone's number one draft choice.

Along with the Coach Bryant association, that report was a major force in getting the Jets to draft me. That the Jets had a Pittsburgh connection gave me a level of comfort that is hard to explain. The only sour note from that west coast trip was that the Jets got crushed 38-3 by the Chargers. But Mr. Werblin backed his team 100%. The Jets were the best, no matter the score. I liked that.

St. Louis certainly didn't ask me to come watch them. In fact, Mike told me that they kept delaying their bids. Mike would call them, tell them what

Mr. Werblin had bid, and then it would take a day or two for them to respond. Later, I heard that St. Louis was bidding for the New York Giants, who didn't want their cross-town rivals to beat them in a high profile signing. St. Louis went up to $400,000, but there were all sorts of conditions in the contract—they wanted me to host some radio show or something in addition to playing football. And in the end, they threw their cards on the table and asked if I'd be willing to play for the Giants.

That kind of hustling didn't sit well with me. The NFL had great players. But everybody seemed to wear their hair a certain way and live up to a very arbitrary code of "conduct." They didn't seem to have the liberty to be themselves.

I can just imagine how the NFL would have reacted to my white shoes. My feet just felt lighter in white. So I wore white shoes. I couldn't understand why people made a big deal out of it. And the more I noticed that everyone else wore black shoes and the more people wanted me to change, the less interest I had in conforming. I didn't get any conditions from Mr. Werblin. In fact, he was probably the guy responsible for a fresh pair of white shoes waiting for me in my first Jet locker. He liked me the way I was. He liked my story. The NFL didn't. Simple as that.

So, Mike worked the rest out with Mr. Werblin and I gave him my word that I would sign the Jets contract right after the Orange Bowl. I would receive a salary of $25,000 per year for three years guaranteed. (That's about $315,000 a year in today's money, a third more than the 2005 NFL league minimum of $230,000 per year.) And I received a $200,000 signing bonus ($2,500,000 in today's money), which would not begin to be paid out until I completed my three-year contract.

The total was $300,000, which I thought was a good deal for Mr. Werblin (his initial offer) and for me. Of course, he had to throw in a brand new Jet green Lincoln Continental, which cost another $7,000.

So how did a guy making an annual salary less than the Oiler's Billy Cannon ($25,000 versus $30,000) become the $400,000 quarterback? As I said, Mr. Werblin knew about stars and stories, and this hustle brought me inside his world.

Together, we figured out a way to give him what he needed—a great story to sell Jets tickets—and me what I wanted—to take care of the important people in my life. First Mr. Werblin agreed that the Jets would pay Mike's $30,000 agent fee (10% of $300,000) and he agreed to hire three football scouts who I recommended, namely Bob Namath, Frank Namath, and Tommy Sims (my brother-in-law) at $10,000 a year each for three years guaranteed. So the whole Jets package came to $427,000.

When were figuring out this deal, you'll notice my mother was not a part of this arrangement. Brother Bob got upset about that after I explained what I had worked out with the Jets. I remember Bob saying, "Well, what about Mom?"

It totally came out of left field because mom would be taken care of. I was shocked. I was caught up in the excitement of being able to come home with that news and say look what we can do! I though everyone would be happy. But no, Brother Bob smacked me down again because I'd forgotten about Mom. I really felt hurt that he thought that I'd forgotten that. Of course Mom will be taken care of! Are you kidding me?

While driving out of Tuscaloosa for what seemed to be the last time, I thought, "Wow, what a difference this is compared to my arrival four years ago." I made an agreement with myself, and my spirit, to try never to do anything that I'd have to look over my shoulder for again. Worry about how I did something. Worry about how I behaved.

Whether it was siphoning gas, reselling junk from the junk yard, or lifting pop bottles from back porches. I was trying to find a way. Now I had such a good head start, I shouldn't make those kinds of choices again. Because those mistakes all seemed to come from trying to get ahead. And they seemed to be based on making ends meet. Two hundred—excuse me!—400 grand, you know. It was more than I could ever even imagine. I thought, "Boy, if you ever have to look over your shoulder again, you are a real dope."

Now at the Toots Shor's party, Dr. Nicholas walked up to me in the middle of all the schmoozing and introduced himself. He had this cheery smiling Greek face and he said, "Hello. My name is Dr. Jim Nicholas."

I said, "How do you do?"

He gave me a smile and said, "I'm the Jets' orthopedist. I hear you have a bad knee." And he smiled again.

I said, "Yes sir."

He said, "I need to see it."

And I said, "Okay. When do you want to see it?"

And he smiled again and said, "Now."

So we walked into the men's room. And I dropped my pants. We got out of the way of the traffic but we're standing there where anybody could see us in the men's room foyer and I'm standing there with my pants down to my ankles now. He's down on his knees examining my knee. A guy came in gave us a look and made a U-turn. I don't know what he was thinking, but he split.

Anyway, that's where I got my first physical from the New York Jets. Dr. Nicholas had me in the hospital soon after. It only took him one look, and he said, "We gotta do this…immediately."

Many years later, Dr. Nicholas and I were visiting in his office and he smiled and he looked over and he said, "You know, Joe, today the way we do things, we wouldn't have even drafted you."

I smiled back and said, "Well, that would've been a big mistake!"

After our men's room rendezvous, Dr. Nick pulled Head Coach Weeb Ewbank aside and said, "Hope we've got another quarterback." A writer from

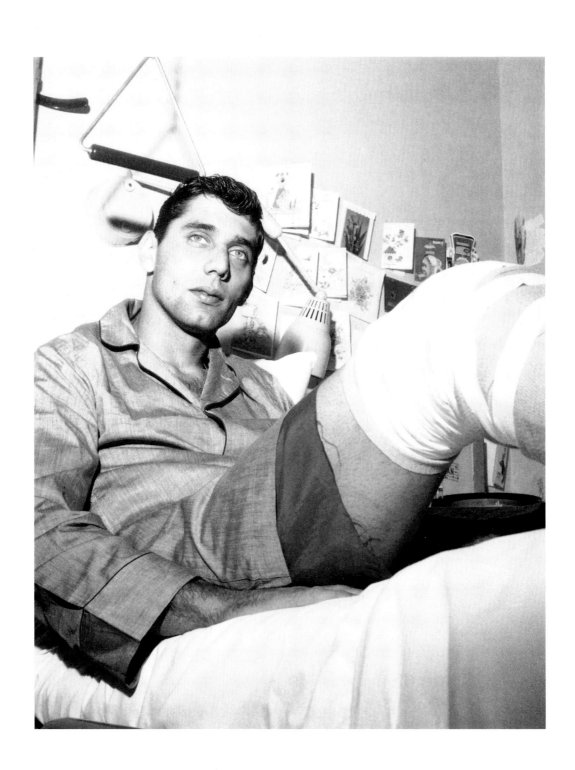

the *New York Times* must have overheard him. After two hours of grilling about my contract, he snickered something like, "Hey kid, suppose you don't make it? What happens to the money?"

"I'll make it."

Mr. Werblin now had his story—wounded, over hyped and overpaid quarterback against all odds, is he as good as he says he is? And I had the starring role. Now, all I had to do was check into Lenox Hill Hospital that Sunday night, have my leg sliced open, my medial meniscus removed, my medial collateral ligament doubled back on itself and stapled, then rebuild that leg in six months. After that, I had to beat out the Jets current quarterback (Mike Taliafierro) and the 1964 Heisman trophy winner (John Huarte had been signed as insurance for over $200,000) for the starting job. Then I had to deal with my military draft status (1965 was a build-up year in Vietnam), before I played one down. No problem. I was going to be 22 years old in May.

If you have never had knee surgery, it's hard to explain just how disturbing it is to wake up and have your leg hurt more after the operation than it did before. As with many things in this world, things get worse before they get better. And Dr. Nicholas had me rehabbing that leg before I even got back to my room. Like in the post-operative recovery area.

When I opened my eyes, my brothers were there. And Dr. Nick's great Ernest Borgnine kind of smile greeted me. He started explaining to me how everything went well and that I'd have to start exercising.

I nodded.

"I mean, Joe, right now." He picked up my leg, which had a cast on it from the ankle up to the top of my thigh, "Now, what I want you to do, Joe is to tense up your quadriceps muscle. Here. Now you gotta keep working that muscle." He was holding the heel and said, "Now, I'm going to let go of this

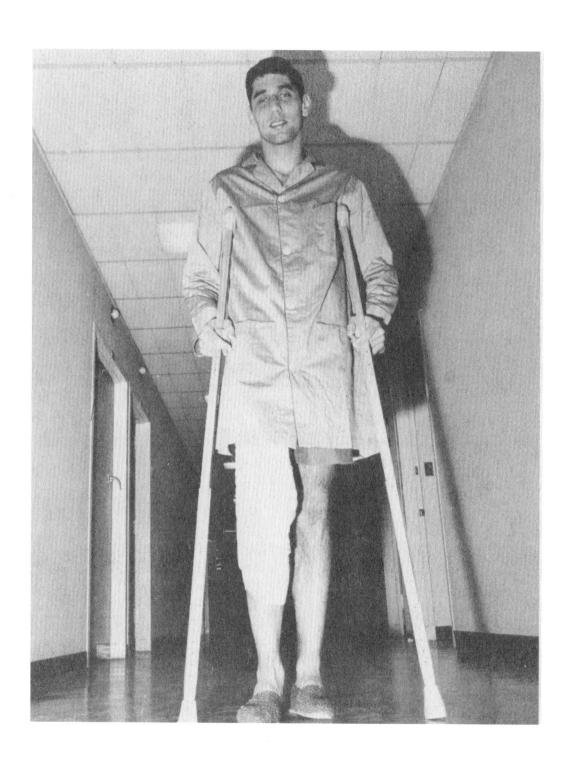

and you hold that leg up there and this is how you've got to start exercising. You've got to work."

And he let go of that heel. I had to hold that cast up because my brothers were there. I'd have never held it up for any other reason. I mean, it hurt! But, I knew that if he's asking me do it, I must be able to do it. Or at least try. I don't know if I could've done it, I don't know if I would've cared enough, if they weren't there.

Dr. Nick was very happy, though. He said, "Joe, the operation went really well, it's great, we think you can play four years." I remember thanking God that I could play pro football for four years. Maybe.

Mr. Werblin had a photographer from *Sports Illustrated* in the operating room—they ran a four-page feature on my operation in February 1965. A master at turning out a story, Mr. Werblin knew the importance of having the media on his side. Not by accident, there was an open-door policy to our locker room. And all press rode in the first-class section on the Jet charter planes while the team sat back in coach. *SI* must have sold a lot of that February issue, because on July 19 they put me on the cover at the intersection of

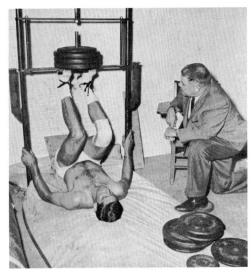

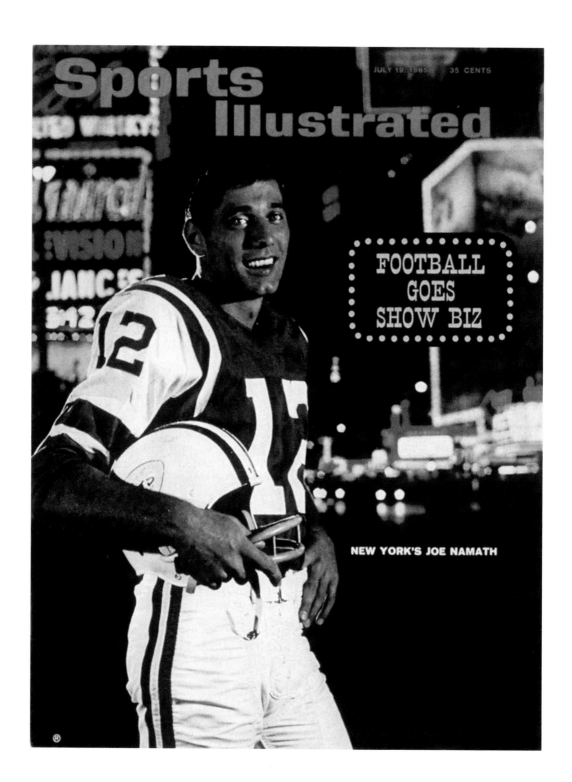

Broadway and Seventh Avenue, the same place where James Dean was pictured in the rain in that photo called the "Boulevard of Broken Dreams." By the time training camp rolled around, the $400,000 quarterback with the bum leg story had sold about 35,000 more Jets season tickets. At about $40 a pop, Mr. Werblin's investment was worth a cool $1,400,000, even if my knee buckled. I guess the guys at Toots' weren't very good at math.

When I showed up for training camp at Peekskill Military Academy on July 14, 1965, I didn't pull up in my shiny new Lincoln Continental. I took Weeb's advice and caught a ride from a photographer for *Life* magazine who wanted pictures of me for another profile. Jets training camp accommodations

were a far cry from Paul W. Bryant Hall and the comforts of southern cooking. If I had any doubt that pro football was a business, I sure learned fast. The rooms had no air conditioning, nor bug screens for that matter. I roomed with my competition, Mike Taliaferro and John Huarte. It was awful.

On Rookie Night when it was my turn to sing the Alabama fight song, "Yea, Alabama," I was drowned out by Bake Turner and the veterans singing "There's No Business Like Show Business" instead. It couldn't have been more obvious that the star system was a problem for the team—the attention, the money, and my inflated reputation.

The $400,000 quarterback may help to sell seats at Shea Stadium, but it put me in line for some problematic practices. Veteran linebackers Larry Grantham and Wahoo McDaniel weren't too happy about some snot-nose kid coming in as the owner's pet project. So I took my lumps in practice, ignored the late hits, and kept my mouth shut.

All of the publicity aside, you can't fake it in football. It's a team game, but reliant on individual performances. I had to earn the respect of everyone on that team in order to have the opportunity to perform. Playing for Coach Bryant gave me great football credentials. Every player in pro football knew that you couldn't play for Coach Bryant without owning up. And there were two other guys in camp who knew what I could do first hand. Jim Hudson and George Sauer, Jr. Hud was the Texas quarterback who defeated Alabama in the Orange Bowl and he'd come to camp as a defensive strong safety. George Sauer, Jr., also a Longhorn, was the wide receiver that caught Hud's 69-yard touchdown pass. Hud would end up as one of my closest friends on the team and my road roommate, for a while, anyway. Like me, George took his lumps too, as his dad was a higher-up in the Jets organization and many on the team thought he won his spot in camp as a favor. He would turn out to be one of the all-time Jet greats.

While I learned the Jet offense, I was also dealing with my 1-A military draft status. Having left college and its automatic deferment, I was now in at the front of the line for Vietnam. Now I grew up with the understanding that all young men in the United States were expected to serve their country. My oldest brother John fought in both the Korea and Vietnam wars and he made a good life for himself as a career soldier. I was proud to be a part of that tradition and I followed the book when it came time to have my physical for induction.

But on account of the damage to my knee, I was designated unfit for military service.

After the press reports came out that I'd failed my medical exam for induction, I received some really stupid, vicious letters, and some were even sent to my mother, telling her I was a draft dodger and worse. I've said it before and I'll say it again. I dutifully went through three examinations by different military orthopedic specialists to verify the initial finding.

If I said I was glad, I was a traitor. If I said I was disappointed, I would have been a fool. Kids in college were getting deferments, married guys were getting deferments, people wondered how a football player, a professional athlete nonetheless, could get a deferment.

In 1969 after we'd won the Super Bowl, I went on a U.S.O. tour in the Far East, I visited with recovering soldiers in various hospitals. Some were as young as or younger than I was, with awful injuries that reminded me of how lucky I was with my minor knee problem. I hurt my knee on a football field on a beautiful fall day with thousands of fans concerned about me. Our soldiers were sacrificing themselves on distant fields with no one there to inspire them. I'll never forget those injured soldiers. God bless them.

Just before we broke camp my Rookie year, this veteran linebacker jumped on me as we were running a lap before practice had ended and I fell down. I had a quick word with him on the field, and afterward the team had a "players only" meeting. It was a Jet tradition to clear the air before the season began and the team felt it was time. We had to play together, put the game together on the field. After a few of the guys stood up and said what they had to say, our offensive captain Mike Hudock, said, "Anybody else wanna say anything?"

I felt like I had to stand up and say something. "If you don't like me, do something now, come on, stand up, tell me, and we'll get something straight somehow. You might whip me, but you're gonna get a fight."

Surprisingly no one did stand up, including the linebacker who jumped me. I said that we had to win as a team. I didn't care if they didn't like me off the field. I could live with that. The bottom line was what we did together on the field.

When September rolled around, I was on the bench, manning the phones in an opening season loss to the Houston Oilers in Houston. The fact of the matter was that Mile Taliaferro was playing at a higher level then I was at the time. It was excruciating to sit, and I was anxious to play.

Weeb was getting heavy pressure from Mr. Werblin to start me. Now as most coaches will tell you, there is no let-up from owners, but if a coach ends up losing his credibility with his players, he's lost his team. Weeb, always mindful of that and despite his nickname "The Jolly Green Midget," was no one's fool. The man groomed Johnny Unitas. I could wait my turn.

It came the following week, at home. Weeb put me in front of Mr. Werblin's sell-out crowd (he was no dummy either) in the second quarter against Kansas City. I hit Don Maynard for my first pro touchdown, but we lost 14-10. The rest of the season is a blur. I played well enough to be named the AFL's Rookie of the Year and we had our moments as a team, but we were a long way from a championship. We finished with 5 wins, 8 losses, and 1 tie.

CHAPTER 06 The Long-Haired Hard Hat

The Unavoidable Hard Work of Professional Football

It took a while to hone the Jet passing offense. I knew a thing or two about offenses, having learned the basics under two outstanding head coaches, Coach Bruno and Coach Bryant. Both men believed that the quarterback was their representative on the field and that if they trained him right, stressing his footwork fundamentals and artful faking, giving him the right plays against each opponent, teaching him the opponent's defensive coverages and blitz packages, and then poring over the game plan with him before each game, that he would have what he needed to call his own plays.

The advantages of having a quarterback capable of calling his own game are enormous. Because he has an on-the-field perspective, he can see and feel exactly how the defense is reacting to each and every play call. There are just times when you know as a player when you can beat your man, when your opponent's unsure, or when he does not want you to go his way. If your quarterback is calling the plays, he can listen to the input of his teammates, ask them questions, and generally exploit these weaknesses in the moment. But the quarterback has to control the huddle. I can remember one time, having to threaten to call a time out because of two guys arguing with one another in the huddle—our center John Schmitt and our guard Dave Herman—they were arguing about something up front. And I told them to get quiet, and then I asked them in a nice way, "Are we gonna have to waste a timeout on you guys?" I mean, really, because that's what it amounts to.

But teammates have plenty to share with a quarterback—just not in the huddle. If I know that the middle linebacker is nursing a bad ankle and cannot move to his right, I call a running play directly at his point of weakness and we keep running it until he stops it, is pulled out of the game, or we score a touchdown.

In today's game, with the exception of audibles (play changes at the line of scrimmage), quarterbacks do not call their own plays. The plays are wired to them through a speaker in their helmets from coaches on the sidelines. We didn't have that back then. What 1960s and 1970s pro head coaches relied on were their quarterbacks having the experience and presence of mind to anticipate what the other team was going to do, before they did it. Not all of those coaches gave their quarterbacks this kind of authority. Some would "shuttle" in plays with wide receivers, guards, or other substitutes before each play. Paul Brown with the Cleveland Browns and Tom Landry with the Dallas Cowboys continued to insist on calling plays. I might add that they did pretty well, too. But when a head coach found a quarterback that he had confidence in to call his own game, he was damn happy to have him. It gave that coach an edge. And edges win football games.

I never knew any other way to play. Play-calling was always a large part of the thrill for me. Outsmarting or out-guessing the other team with a perfect play call was just as cool as throwing a bomb. Getting the chance to call my own plays in high school was a great education, and looking back now, I see that Coach Bruno took a real chance when he gave me that job. He was only in his second year coaching Beaver Falls and putting his faith in a 17-year-old kid could not have been easy. But great coaches recognize what will drive a team to a win. Watching my brothers play from my earliest years, playing hour after hour with my pals in the playground, and living and studying the game in my mind gave me the smarts to smell an opponent's weakness. Somehow Coach Bruno and later Coach Bryant knew what I could do with my mind as well as what I could do with my arms and legs. That's not to say that they didn't disagree with some of my decisions and chew me out over mental mistakes, but I honestly can't remember them beating me up over play-calling. We had the one-eyed monster, our film projector, and we'd go through every decision before and after every game. You can't BS the one-eyed monster.

Like Coach Bruno and Coach Bryant Weeb Ewbank was also a believer in the quarterback being the on-field general. But his demeanor and motivational strategies were something else entirely. He coached grown men and knew that men needed more than "the old college try" or the fear of a father figure to lay it all out on the field. The pro game is a cold-blooded business. And Weeb knew that first hand.

Don't get me wrong, playing pro football is a great job. Maynard used to say, "I'm gonna keep playing till they run me off, or carry me outta here. I'll stay as long as I can." And he wasn't the only one who appreciated the opportunity. I remember a young player telling me at a golf tournament in Lake Tahoe about how lucky he felt to be in the league. He was going to play as long as anyone wanted him—Dan Marino. I think Brett Favre knows what a special job it is, too.

Wilbur Charles Ewbank grew up in a small Indiana town, Richmond, and despite being on the small side, played semi-pro football and baseball to support

his young wife Lucy and family while attending Miami of Ohio University (Ben Roethlisberger's alma matter) and earning his degree. After graduating, he got a job as a teacher and assistant coach at a high school in Van Wert, Ohio. He then moved to McGuffey High School in Oxford, Ohio as head coach and spent thirteen years compiling a 71-21 record, winning 21 straight at one point and never having a losing season.

During World War II, the 36-year-old Weeb headed to the Great Lakes Naval Training Center for a three-year hitch. There he met the legendary Paul

Brown and served as his assistant coach for the camp's team along with my brother Frank's coach at Kentucky, Blanton Collier. When he was discharged from the Navy, he continued coaching, and eventually was hired by Paul Brown as his assistant at the Cleveland Browns. During his time in Cleveland, the Browns won either the divisional championship or league championship throughout Weeb's five-year tenure.

The Baltimore Colts' owner Carroll Rosenbloom hired Weeb as head coach in 1954. He got the job by guaranteeing Rosenbloom a championship in five years. And when he brought in Johnny Unitas in 1956 for a tryout, he was only two years away. In 1958, the Colts beat the Giants in the game that turned pro football into a national phenomenon. Weeb won it again with the Colts in 1959. Then after a 7-7 season in 1962, Mr. Rosenbloom shocked the entire football world by firing him. He gave the head coaching job to one of Weeb's assistants, a young coach in his thirties named Don Shula.

So in early 1963, Weeb was 56 years old and out of a job. With 34 years of coaching experience behind him, plus two NFL championships, Weeb was looking for work. Mr. Werblin knew a great story in the making when he saw one. Weeb Ewbank was a winner, now cast as an underdog. Plus he had a funny name.

When he was introduced as the new coach of the new New York Titans, now renamed the New York Jets, Weeb said, "I've seen sicker cows than this one get well. I had a five-year plan in Baltimore and I don't see why we can't build a winner here in five years." For a team that had exactly one star receiver (Don Maynard), one dominant linebacker (Larry Grantham), one solid halfback (Billy Mathis), and a reliable punter (Curley Johnson), winning anything was pretty big talk.

Weeb had the exact opposite coaching style than Coach Bryant. And it took me a while to get to know him. He didn't have a tower. There was no iron-fisted discipline. And that was for a reason. At the time, I didn't really get it, but now it makes complete sense. Pro football is a game, just like high school and college, but the stakes are much higher. Each guy on the field is no longer playing for the glory of the alma matter. He's not playing for the love of Betty Sue or for "fun" anymore. He's playing to support himself, his family, and his future. The professional head coach has to deal with these facts, and all of the "rah, rah" stuff only goes so far.

Weeb knew a couple of things when he took the Jets job. He knew that he had to win, which was fine by him. That was his job. But he also knew that just winning wouldn't be enough. He won in Baltimore and got fired. He'd have to keep the ownership happy. And that meant keeping the seats filled, keeping his players in line and focused, and making sure that <u>he</u> never became the big story.

This brings me back to the Jets offense, and for that matter, the whole AFL way of playing pro football. Weeb took over the Jets in 1963 and he came into a league that had a "loose" playing style. The AFL disdained the conservative offenses of the NFL. And defensively, the AFL expansively implemented blitzes—secondary blitzes became famous. The NFL was more conservative, and even though there were blips of downfield passers (Sammy Baugh, Otto Graham, and Johnny U.), it was just not as refreshing as the AFL. The AFL was about freedom. And no team was as free as the AFL's Sand Diego Chargers, the team that I saw beat the Jets 38-3 when I was a senior at Alabama.

The Chargers' downfield air attack under another NFL head coach castoff, Sid Gillman, was a thing of beauty. Weeb witnessed it and knew that the future of the game was in the air. He was going to need a quarterback in the mold of Johnny Unitas if he was to deliver on his five-year plan. So while the pro scouting world (including Mr. Werblin) was salivating over college QBs like George Mira of Miami in 1963, Weeb let it be known that he had his eye on a young player who wasn't even available yet for the draft.

As Weeb said, "Well George Mira's really an exciting football player, but I've known for a long time that those great small guys don't win a championship for you. And they're great quarterbacks—Eddie LeBaron, Frankie Albert, Fran Tarkenton—they're great ball-handlers and all that. But we're interested in a championship. The guy that would intrigue us is this junior quarterback at Alabama."

I've since heard that none other than Coach Bryant had given Weeb a scouting report on me and what I might do in the pro game. With this in mind, Weeb set out to draft himself a running game in 1963. He got one in the form of Ohio State star Matt Snell. Matt was a straight, no nonsense man and player. Mr. Werblin closed the deal by bringing his folks some coffee during a cold day at the Polo Grounds. Matt had an offer in from the Giants too, but they insulted him saying that there was no guarantee that he'd even make their club. Mr. Werblin treated him with the respect he deserved. Matt hit the Jets running, teaming up with Bill Mathis in the backfield and winning the AFL rookie of the year award in 1964.

When I hit Peekskill in 1965, next on Weeb's agenda was the air attack. Now, I had a pretty good gun, but another quarterback in camp, returning starter Mike Taliaferro had a stronger one. Weeb and offensive coordinator Clive Rush figured out how best to use a quarterback with the arm strength to go deep downfield. Even though Weeb used the same playbook my whole career, he tweaked our execution. Our plays were basically the same ones he had with the Baltimore Colts, and I wouldn't be surprised if he had copied them from Paul Brown. Creative plays matter little if you can't execute.

There's a picture of Johnny Unitas during the Super Bowl. He's on the sidelines, listening to what I'm calling from the field—audibles. He's actually mouthing the words that I'm calling. The Colts had the same plays we had, the same numbering system!

Weeb changed our pass protection. That change became a critical element of our growth. He believed that our offensive linemen, if they took on their defensive counterparts early, would be able to buy the quarterback a fraction of a second longer to view the field and release the ball. And worst case, the defense would be slowed down in their rush to a point where the quarterback could get rid of the ball before taking a sack.

"Protect the quarterback" was Weeb's main offensive strategy, coming from working and seeing what a great quarterback like Johnny Unitas could do. Even if we had to go to maximum protection (both backs stay in to pass block and sometimes even the tight end) to get the ball downfield, we'd stress protecting the quarterback. I liked that.

It's not really appropriate to compare pass blocking of today to my time because of the rule changes that occurred in the late '70s, allowing offensive linemen to extend their arms and hands when pass blocking. Anyway, the "take them on at the line of scrimmage" blocking was something new and again critical to the success or failure of our passing game. Since I had limited mobility (my scrambling would not result in major Jet gains), that fraction of a second provided by the slow down of the rush was a big deal.

To buy more time for the quarterback, we also dropped the passer back 7 to 10 yards, sometimes deeper. This was a substantial change. Plus, most quarterbacks sidestep; they take crossover steps while dropping back to pass. I never took crossover steps. I would turn and sprint back. When I back-pedaled, it was because I needed to read left. I would also mix that back-pedal in when throwing right from time to time so I didn't type myself with my drop.

As a rookie, training camp had my brain nearly on overload. I was trying to learn this completely new professional offense that Coach Ewbank was teaching, there was major doubt about my knee, plus I wasn't good enough to win the job yet. By the time Weeb did commit to me as the starter, we were in the thick of the 1965 season. I learned on the job. While I was a little early or late with the ball to the receivers during that year, I was picking up a lot in terms of defensive tendencies, coverages, and play-calling. To chalk up the '65 season, just to put it in a nutshell—it wasn't a successful season because we didn't win enough. When you look at the transition and all, it was a reasonably successful year. It ended on a positive note, in the sense that we were looking forward to the next season. We knew we were getting better.

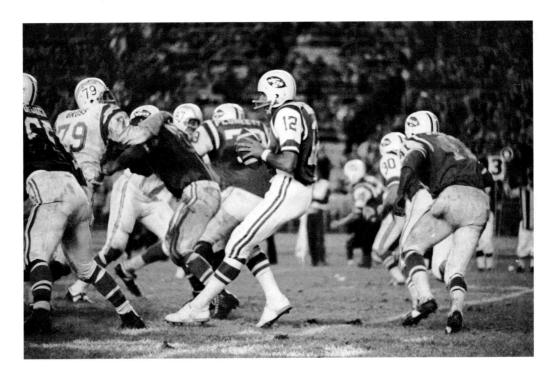

Now, the 1966 Peekskill training camp was really about getting our timing down. Back then, camps began around the early to middle of July and went through early to the middle of September (we played six preseason games, not four), and the daily grind went something like this:

7:00 a.m.	Rise and Shine
7:30 a.m.	Breakfast
8:30 a.m.	Meetings—Reviewing films, charting plays, going over down and distance situations, opposing defenses etc.
9:30 a.m.	On the Field
12:00 p.m.	Lunch
2:00 p.m.	Quarterback Meeting with Coach
3:00 p.m.	Afternoon Practice
6:00 p.m.	Dinner
7:30 p.m.	Meetings until 9:00 p.m.
11:00 p.m.	Curfew—Players must be in their rooms

Fun, huh? Let's just say I missed curfew a time or two and paid my share of fines. But I made sure I put in the hours with my receivers to get down our aerial attack. We'd throw in the morning practice, after the morning practice, in the afternoon practice, and after the afternoon practice. All in all, about three to three and a half hours a day during camp.

Now Don Maynard and George Sauer (two of the best receivers of all time) were very different.

Don, having been through training camps and all, wasn't your eager beaver, all out, 100% practice player. Not with six preseason games to play. He paced himself because he knew no one would take care of him for him. Don had enough confidence in his ability to play to monitor himself at practices. If a coach asked Don to run something, he'd run it if it made sense to him, but not a stupid thing like a 40-yard dash to find out how fast he might be.

George would stay after practice and constantly worked on his footwork and catching the ball. George and I started out together as Rookies, so naturally we worked a lot together and our timing was excellent.

The on-the-field difference begins with Maynard's speed and Sauer's so-called lack of speed, just as hall of famers Fred Biletnikoff and Steve Largent had lack of speed. That was the major difference. The defense had to respect Maynard's speed first, otherwise he'd beat them deep for a touchdown.

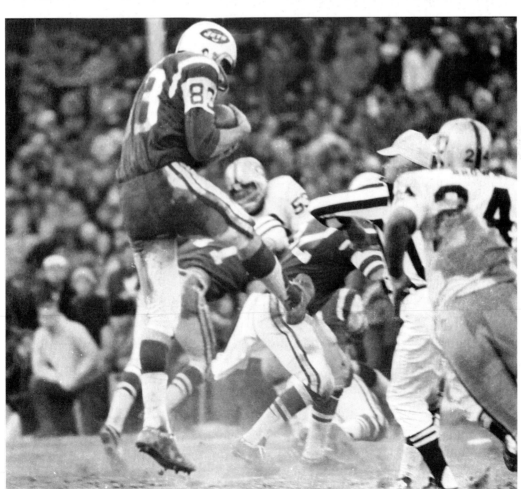

So on the other side, we had a perfect complement in George, who didn't have that lightning speed but was a precision route-runner. George rarely broke a route. Don was somewhat of a free spirit and that carried over into his pass routes. He would simply break his route if he knew he could run by the defender or beat him deep. Together, Maynard and Sauer were a real handful for the defenses to cover. They never knew where Don was going, and George was so tight with his footwork, they'd commit to his first move and I'd hit him on his second or third.

By the time the 1966 season started, we were firing on a lot of cylinders. With almost three hundred yards and five touchdowns coming through the passing game, we opened up the home season against Houston and won 52-13. Believe it or not, the Oilers had a good defense too. They had held Denver without a first down and had shut out the Raiders, so lighting them up really got us going.

After our first five games we were undefeated with over one thousand yards in the air and nine touchdowns. But then, as we began to play the same teams again in the second half of the season, our opponents adjusted their defensive schemes, and I did what quarterbacks have done since the beginning of time. I threw interceptions. We finished the year at 6-6-2. Just after our last game against the Patriots, I went under the knife again to remove more cartilage debris in my right knee and to have a ligament rebuilt from my patella tendon. That surgery would evolve over time to become what is now called an ACL reconstruction.

Weeb had one more year left to bring the Jets a championship and I had six months to rebuild my right leg. Again.

Photo: Harry Benson

CHAPTER 07 | On Broadway

Bringing It All Back Home

I dream in 8mm. Clickity clack, back, clickity clack forward, clickity clack back again, clickity clack. A day or two before Super Bowl III, four of us were riding from the Galt Ocean Mile Hotel out to practice at New York Yankee's Ft. Lauderdale Stadium. Pete Lammons, Vito "Babe" Parilli, Billy Mathis, and I and were talking about the Colts just after watching films at our offensive meeting. Big Boy Pete—I can see him right now, riding shotgun and leaning back—said, "Hey y'all, we keep looking at those films, we're gonna get overconfident." Now, I'd studied game film from Beaver Falls to Tuscaloosa, and if there was one thing I learned, it was that the one-eyed monster didn't lie. And the monster had told me over and over again that the New York Jets could win the Championship.

But only a year and change before, it looked like we were bound for palooka-ville. Coming off that physical beating in Oakland in '67, many thought that Weeb was going to be fired. Even though we had become the AFL's sentimental favorites, we were officially out of the playoffs and his five years were up.

We played hard in San Diego in our last game and won it to close out 1967 at 8-5-1. We went over the 4,000-yard mark for total passing yardage in a 14-game season. At the time we didn't even know that we had broken a record, but now it's nice to look back on. A year that began with so much promise had slowly sunk into another pit of near misses. It was a year that made my knees seem like the strongest on the team. We lost our offensive captain, left guard Sam DeLuca, in the preseason with a torn-up knee. Then Matt Snell blew his knee out in an early game against Buffalo. Then Emerson Boozer, who was leading the league in scoring, ripped up his knee against Kansas City. Our 5-1-1 record start, like 1966 all over again, fell apart. Every game we played without Matt and Boo was an invitation for the defenses to blitz. And blitz they did.

I didn't have a very Merry 1967 Christmas. I went into a full-length cast from thigh to ankle to give my left knee time to heal a chronic case of tendonitis. It had developed from favoring my right knee. That didn't work, so on March 20, 1968, I went back to Lenox Hill. Dr. Nick fixed a small tear on my patella tendon and dug out some cartilage. When I woke up from the latest surgery, my left leg looked like a tooth pick because of atrophy. I had eight weeks to rebuild the leg for training camp.

But for those eight weeks, my left leg was the least of the Jets troubles. I had heard that the Jets ownership was in flux over what Mr. Werblin and I had worked out between us a year before.

At the end of the 1966 season, I came out of knee surgery number two on leg number one (the right one) knowing I was one perfect hit away from retirement. The newspapers still referred to me as the $400,000 quarterback, but there were no guarantees that I'd land another contract. And all of the planning in the world was not going to make that one deal enough for me to live on the rest of my life.

Now, before I ever became a Jet, the Gotham Football Club reported losses of $700,000 in 1963 and $648,000 in 1964. After my rookie year in 1965, they went into the black. To his credit, Mr. Werblin believed that if he had the right star, he'd bring the team into profit. He had and he did.

Another fact of the marketplace was that after my rookie year, the NFL came calling on the AFL to make peace. My contract was among the first of some major wins for players and both leagues knew that they couldn't compete forever. Linebacker Tommy Nobis' $600,000 deal with the Atlanta Falcons was the next to make big news. Even Vince Lombardi, who it has been said once traded a guy who brought in an agent to negotiate his contract, had to open up the coffers. He signed Illinois running back Jim Grabowski, to a whopping $850,000 contract for Green Bay.

The two leagues had a gentlemen's agreement that all was fair in signing rookies, but a cross-league defection by Pete Gogolak from the AFL Buffalo Bills to the NFL New York Giants brought the competition to a head. AFL teams started signing NFL players. NFL teams retaliated. The players loved it. More money was coming our way.

But in June 1966, NFL commissioner Mr. Pete Rozelle worked out a deal with Mr. Lamar Hunt and the two leagues called a truce. In 1970, they would merge. The result of the merger was terrible for players, competitive bidding for pro football players ended right then and there. But he also announced that in the three years leading up to 1970, the champion of the NFL and the champion of the AFL would meet in a World Championship football game at the end of the year. This game would come to be known as the Super Bowl.

So now that the AFL and the NFL weren't competing, there was little chance that I was going to be able to hold up the Jets for fair market value, like players can do today. The reality was that I had one year left on my first contract that covered 1967, plus an option year that the Jets could pick up at $25,000 for 1968. I sincerely did not know if my leg would make it through 1967, so I flew to Miami to see Mr. Werblin and explain my situation.

We worked out a reasonable second contract. It was a no-cut, guaranteed agreement that turned out to be another bargain for the New York Jets. The base for the 1969, 1970 and 1971 seasons was $35,000 a year. I was also to receive a bonus of $10,000 for the 1967 season, a bonus of $25,000 for the 1968 season, and a lump bonus of $150,000 that wasn't due until 1972. I bought my brother Frank's house for my mom up on Patterson Heights in Beaver Falls to celebrate the new agreement. That house is still in the family. It was first owned by my Uncle Joe—my mother's brother—who sold it to Frank, and now one of Frank's children owns it.

After the 1967 season and even up until recently, I didn't think much about that contract extension. I've since learned that a report circulated around town that Mr. Werblin was in a dispute with his partners because he neglected to tell them about our negotiation. The Jets were also owned by Leon Hess, Phil Iselin, Donald Lillis, and Townsend Martin. They had no problem with Mr. Werblin being the managing partner and making these decisions before. They enjoyed their days at Shea Stadium on game day, without having to deal with the headaches during the week. But I guess seeing Mr. Werblin in the paper all the time referred to as "the owner" of the New York Jets started to wear thin on them.

At the time, though, I had heard that Mr. Werblin and Mr. Hess weren't getting along. Before one game, in one of his suites, Mr. Werblin may not have been as polite as he should have been to Mr. Hess. I didn't know that my contract had anything to do with the core argument and I still don't think it did. If anything, they were using it as an excuse to present an ultimatum to Mr. Werblin.

It soon became apparent that one of them had to go. So, like gentlemen, Mr. Hess and Mr. Werblin decided to blindly bid for the other's shares. Whoever agreed to pay more would buy the other out. Mr. Hess offered more money than Mr. Werblin did. And that's how Mr. Hess became the Jets majority owner. Eventually Mr. Hess bought out the other shareholders too. What happened between the two men remained a private issue.

Now when Donald Lillis found out about the contract extension, it's been reported that he went through the roof. And after Mr. Werblin left (May 1968), he became the new managing partner. He knew that Weeb's contract had run dry and many said that he was determined to take control quickly and put his stamp on the team.

He tried to lure Vince Lombardi to the Jets, offering him just about anything he wanted. It wasn't enough. But Mr. Lillis' tenure did not last long. To the team's shock, he died of a heart attack just as training camp got into swing at our new headquarters on Long Island, New York's Hofstra University.

Some off-season. Phil Iselin agreed to step in as managing partner and he wisely left Weeb alone. He gave him a one-year deal, but let it be known that if he didn't win the Eastern Division championship in 1968, he'd be gone. For the first time in Weeb's tenure with the Jets, he now had complete control over the locker room. The first thing he did was limit the media access and put the trainers' room off-limits.

So we're heading to the Houston Astrodome for a preseason game and Weeb asked me to suit up. I had hurt my knees twice before playing in preseason games and with the doctor's consent, I told Weeb I wasn't playing. He said that's okay, just put on your uniform. I didn't feel that was a good idea because I could mislead the crowd into thinking that I would play. I didn't wear the uniform. Weeb wasn't happy and I wasn't happy.

The next day, a reporter wrote that I refused to play because they weren't paying me enough money for the preseason game and that the team was distracted by my disagreement with Weeb. Actually, because of the swelling in my right knee, we had known the previous Wednesday that I wouldn't play.

Anyway, the day before the opener at Kansas City following a light practice, Weeb called us together on the field and he announced the outcome of the team's vote for captains. "Defensive captain—Johnny, Johnny Sample, you're the defensive captain." And right away, I thought, "Wow, isn't that something," because Johnny was a free spirit and we all appreciated his work ethic. He was all business on the field.

"And Joe, you're the offensive captain." I felt stunned. After a while, Curley Johnson, our veteran jack-of-all-trades told me the guys wanted me to have more responsibility. They figured that making me captain would help me to own up, or something. I thought Curley was kidding me. Being elected captain, to me, is the most flattering thing a ball player can achieve. Getting a vote from a guy shows that he likes your work ethic.

Next to being on a championship team, it's the best honor a player can earn. Beating the Chiefs the next day was a huge start to the '68 season. We needed a late drive to seal it and started out on our own one-yard line. We held the ball for over six minutes to keep Hall of Fame kicker Jan Stenerud off the field.

It was great. We'd gained two yards on first down. Second down, I checked to a quick post for Maynard, but I missed him. I was so angry at myself, knowing it was there, and I went right back to Don with the same play. We hit it! First down. We get to another third down and I hit George on the left side for another first down. We kept the ball for over six minutes to finish off the chiefs and I remember hearing Hank Stram, Kansas City's coach, saying he never thought any team could do that to his defense.

Following the Kansas City win, we took Boston 47-31. Then went up to Buffalo to play the Bills. I threw seven touchdowns that day, but only four for the Jets. The other three went to Buffalo, and we lost 37-35. The next week our all-pro defensive end Gerry Philbin kindly reminded me in practice that we were wearing green jerseys in the upcoming game. In other words, throw it to the right team, Joe.

We recovered and beat San Diego at Shea to get back on track in October.

The following week we had Denver coming to town, but it poured all week. It was so wet that we never set foot on the field. We practiced in the corridors of Shea Stadium, on the cement floor where they sell the popcorn and hot dogs. I remember coach Ewbank, coming around, worrying about the game because he thought our timing would be off. And I can remember telling him, "Don't worry, Coach. We'll be all right." I threw five interceptions that day and we lost 21-13. I threw 17 interceptions for the year, and 10 of them happened in those two losses to Buffalo and Denver.

We're 3-2 and really not looking like a good, consistent team, or like a consistently good team. We've got a strong defense, some outstanding talent on offense, and we're losing games, just out of stupidity, making mistakes. So Verlon Biggs, one of our defensive ends, decided that he wasn't going to shave until we clinched the division championship.

Something that unrelated to football may not seem like much, but what Verlon did brought us together. There might have been some real angry people on the defensive side of the ball after I threw 10 interceptions, and we lost to the two last-placed teams in the league. But unity was more important than defense versus offense. And with guys on the defense—John Elliot, Cornell Gordon, and Jim Hudson—and guys from the offense—Bake Turner, and myself—deciding to join Verlon in the no-shaving club, we were gonna get through this together.

There was an additional point that Verlon was making to the whole professional football world. We were both men and football players. We were men first, though. And the corny stuff of telling men that they couldn't have beards and mustaches or grow hair, like in the NFL, was flat-out stupid. We were the American Football League's Jets, not the NFL's. Let's grow some hair and be ourselves.

I decided to go with the Fu Manchu. And I spent even more time with the one-eyed monster. After the Denver and Buffalo losses, I reviewed more film and took what the opposing defenses were giving me. Our team had the best defense in the league. Why not let those eleven do their thing and give them the shot to win some games for us? We did, and they did.

We won the next four games. I threw for zero touchdowns and we were in control of our own destiny at 7-2. We headed back to Oakland for a nationally televised game on NBC, a rematch of the broken cheek game. We took it to the Raiders hard and they fought right back. There were over 30 penalties called. At last, we pulled ahead with a little more than a minute left in the game, 32-29. And then NBC pulled the plug to broadcast the classic children's movie *Heidi*.

If there is ever a course of study offered in a university about professional sports, the *Heidi* game would mark the point when the United States became officially crazy for football. Because what happened after NBC turned off the feed with a minute and change left would not have happened if the New York Giants were playing the Pittsburgh Steelers. The NFL just didn't have the kind of excitement that AFL teams delivered.

This was a game between two teams with a short but bloody history. Both teams were part of a league that got no respect. The Oakland Raiders came back and scored two touchdowns in sixty-five seconds and won the game 43-32. As they were scoring, so many fans had flooded NBC's switchboard to complain about losing the broadcast for *Heidi* (10,000 in the first hour alone) that the Circle-7 exchange in the heart of Manhattan's telephone system blew out. Years later I ended up working with the guy that physically pushed the button, Dick Kline.

The first thing he said to me when we met was, "I'm sorry." I said, "Don't be, we lost."

But, the Jets were for real. The *Heidi Bowl* would turn out to be the first game of a trilogy of games that took professional football from Major League Baseball's kid brother to America's sport. MLB could be the national pastime; football was its game, man.

We may have lost to the Raiders, but the rest of the regular season, we ran the table. We beat San Diego 37-15, Miami 35-15, Cincinnati 27-14, and Miami again 37-7. We were the AFL's Eastern Division Champions. Weeb got a new contract. He then pulled out a letter he had received from the AFL commissioner demanding that the rebel Jets shave their rebel hair. The commissioner had sent it to him six weeks earlier at the first sign of visible facial hair. But we were winning! You don't have to do it other people's way when you're winning. Weeb knew his team better then anyone else and he stuck by us.

I thought the whole business with the hair was ridiculous. They weren't allowing us to be ourselves, express ourselves as individuals. We were the AFL man, what's with the NFL stiffness? I asked my agent Jimmy Walsh to see if anyone would pay me to shave. If I was going to shave, I might as well make a buck doing it. Jimmy pulled in ten grand for the commercial from Schick Razors. Talk about having your cake and eating it too.

And best of all, we got our rematch. We'd face the Raiders for the AFL championship in New York.

Game day it was nasty cold. Nearly freezing, with 40-mile–an-hour gusts of wind through Shea at 1 p.m. kickoff, it felt like being at Ice Station Zebra. The field looked like something out of an old Western. Some grass and a lot of dust. It was an awful day. No, I didn't like the weather.

It would start and end with Jet touchdowns, but the game was never in hand. We were 1-5-1 in the last seven games against the Raiders and had to do something different. We opened up with an offensive formation that we hadn't used before. We went to four wide-outs.

On that kind of day, that strategy was something. Even with the wind blowing footballs all over the place in warm-ups, we wanted them to play man coverage. We believed that our receivers could beat them one-on-one and that our offensive line and halfbacks could hold off their pass rush pressure. So how did we get them to do it? We spread it out. And if they didn't take the bait, then we'd run Matt.

With our double-slots, we ended up throwing the ball 49 times. The Raiders did, too.

After the Raiders won the toss and took the ball, we took the wind at our backs. Our defense, which was just brilliant at bending but not breaking, forced a punt. In four plays, I hit Maynard on a 14-yard corner pattern to make it 7-0. Then we got a field goal and led 10-0 at the end of the first quarter. So far so good.

With the wind, Daryl Lamonica drove the Raiders 80 yards, hitting Fred Biletnikoff (from good old Erie PA) for a 29-yard touchdown pass to begin the second quarter. We got another field goal from Jim Turner to go up 13-7 after some great running by Matt Snell. They matched our field goal with one from George Blanda. At the end of the half, we led 13-10.

What you don't see in the box score is that the first half of the AFL Championship game was one of the toughest physical and mental trials I've ever endured. If it weren't for my teammates and my family, I probably would have pulled a Duran against Sugar Ray… "No mas, no mas." Quitting sure did cross my mind. I just didn't feel like going on. But I had something driving me inside. I wasn't taught to live that way. And what it was couldn't be turned off.

Being capable of performing under stress is not a genetic trait. It's environmental. And what I learned at home is what guided me in this game. I didn't think about myself, I thought of my brothers.

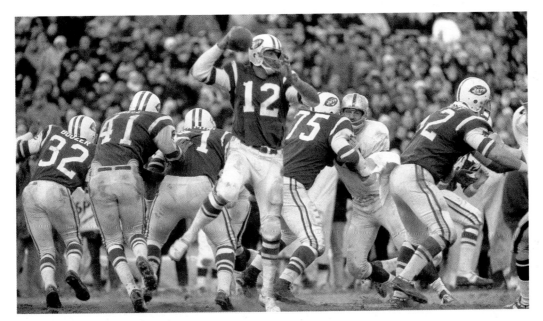

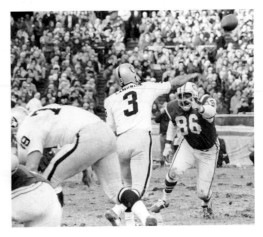

In the first quarter, Ike Lassiter hit me in the head. A gold flash, some smelling salts and I went back out there. Paul Zimmerman, a writer for the *New York Post* at the time, described Lassiter standing over me "like a gladiator waiting for Nero to give the thumb-down sign." It would have been so easy to quit after that concussion. It was so cold that day. I mean, my fingers were numb. It was just not a lot of fun. Football's supposed to be fun. You're supposed to be enjoying it. I wasn't.

In the second quarter, in a pile up, someone dislocated my middle finger on my left hand. It's wonderful what happens on the field. I had thrown a pass, and defensive tackle Dan Birdwell, who just craved to hit quarterbacks, hit me. And I had this pain as he fell on me, while I tried to keep him off. And then my hand hurt. Birdwell got up pointing to it. I got a glance of it and quickly turned away.

Birdwell was so excited, jumping up and down, "Hey, Joe, you broke your finger! You broke your finger!" The enthusiasm! It was third down on that pass, so it was fourth down now. I just ran off the field and over to trainer Jeff Snedeker. I wouldn't look. He just popped my finger back into joint.

So, by halftime, man—aye, aye, aye.

These were the days when your pain-killing injections were common. I missed the halftime speech because I was in the training room with Dr. Nicholas. He shot up both knees, then the dislocated finger. Now, the only times I didn't play in my career, I physically couldn't play. My body just didn't work. But now, I could play. I had to, even if I didn't want to.

Weeb came in and looked at me. I'm lying there, collecting myself, and he didn't say anything. He just stared at me, balled up his fists and made some noises. Then he turned and walked out. I'm not sure exactly sure what it meant, but boy it felt like he was willing me back out there.

Early in the second half, Jim Hudson made three straight tackles on the Jet 6-yard line to stop a Raiders drive. They kicked a field goal instead and tied it at 13.

We got the ball back and drove it down their throats. On a bootleg left, off a fake run-off right tackle, just as I came out of the fake, Ben Davidson had me in his sights. Pete Lammons, our tight end, still had his back to me. So, I actually had to throw around Ben before Pete made his break. But the timing was perfect.

I let it go. Then Davidson was all over me. When Pete made his break the ball was right in front of him. And he just wiped off free safety Dave Grayson and went on into the end zone for the touchdown. Now we had a 20-13 lead going into the fourth quarter.

The fourth opened with Blanda adding a field goal for Oakland. 20-16. We needed a touchdown to seal it, and I went to Maynard to begin the drive with the same corner route that he ran for the touchdown in the first quarter. As I threw the ball, I didn't release it right and the wind ate it up. I saw it fluttering out there, and as my momentum carried me to the left sideline, George Atkinson, their cornerback, cut under Maynard and intercepted the pass. I was already making my way to the sidelines to cut him off and was able to knock him out of bounds at our 2-yard line. Atkinson started running his mouth, "I hate you, I hate you, I hate you." "Shut up, rookie!" I told him, "Just shut up and play the game."

Fullback Pete Banaszak took it in for the Raiders, and we were now behind for the first time in the game, 23-20.

We got the ball back on our own 32-yard line after a terrific effort by our return man, Earl Christy. There were more than eight minutes left in the game. Plenty of time. Take what they give you.

Don Maynard, about three series earlier, came to me on the sideline, "Joe, any time you need it, I can get by him." So, after Oakland scored, I

remembered Don's warrant and told the defense we'd get it back. Now in the huddle, I said, "I'm gonna call two plays, so be alert for the audible. Now listen, if they're playing deep zone, we'll run a 74, but if they are man-to-man tight, I'm gonna change to 60 G."

When we came up to the line of scrimmage, the Oakland cornerbacks, Willie Brown and Atkinson, were laid off about eight yards from the line. They were protecting against the deep ball and stopped playing in their normal tight bump-and-run positions. So, we went with the first play I had called. George caught the 74 underneath and gained 12 yards...boom. We get back in the huddle. I called another play and alert 'em again, "If I see bump and run, we're gonna go 60." We come up to the line with another 74 or 76, and start to get ready. Atkinson then climbs tight up on Maynard and Brown climbs up on Sauer. I checked off with the audible to 60 G.

Maynard was special. You couldn't listen to all receivers. They all thought they were open more times than not. But when Don could get a step on 'em, he knew he could get a step on 'em.

There were three things that might happen with the 60 G:

a) a big Jet completion,

b) an interference call on the Raiders that would give us a big gain, or

c) I'd throw it away incomplete.

I wasn't going to get sacked. What did happen was one of the greatest catches in pro football history.

We were on the left hash mark (they were 10 yards wider than they are now) It was a long, cross-the-field throw. The wind would have time to put some moves on the ball. It was supposed to fall just over Don's right shoulder. He was running at his fastest speed (at least a 4.4 sprinter), even though he wouldn't let anybody clock him. The man covering him, George Atkinson, still high from his interception, maybe even a little cocky, was *only* a step behind. Don turned around at the last instant (we're talking milliseconds here) and saw that the ball had moved from his left to over his right shoulder. He stretched out as far as he could and made the great catch. A helpless Atkinson knocked him out of bounds, piling on top of him.

We were on the Raiders 6 yard line.

The next play was inspired by a New York cab driver that frequented my restaurant, Bachelor's III. After just about every game, he'd come in and give me the business about being too conservative around the goal line.

"Run, run, pass, kick...over and over. Mix it up, for crying out loud." Maybe he was right.

I figured they were expecting a running play, like the cab driver was, so I called a play action pass. I faked the hand-off to Snell off left tackle, and then looked to my first receiver HB Billy Mathis. He was to run a short arrow route to the left front flag of the end zone. George Sauer was my next read, running the short-post route from left to right. Our tight end Pete Lammons was my third option, running a cross pattern right to left. Maynard was my last choice.

Don was to run a square-in from the right deep side of the end zone crossing left.

The problem was the hack was wrong. Everyone was covered and a heavy rush bore down on me. Even if I wanted to throw the ball to the left—Billy was covered, and then I saw George covered. Then Pete…nothing.

But Maynard, being the actor that he was, knew the play's progressions as well as I did. He knew how long it would take for me to get to him, so he was just fooling around; acting like he wasn't doing much until he sensed it was time to break.

With Lassiter, Birdwell, and Davidson gaining ground, my leg slipped out from me on a chunk of dirt in the infield. In that instant, I caught sight of Maynard in the back of the end zone toying with Atkinson. I pivoted to my right and snapped a tight spiral on a line about three feet off of the ground. Either he would catch it or no one would.

He did.

In three plays and thirty-seven seconds of game clock, we had our lead back. Jets 27, Raiders 23. But there were still more then seven minutes left to play.

The rest of the game belonged to our defense. Verlon Biggs sacked Lamonica in a crucial fourth down to stop the next Raider drive.

Our offense burned some clock, but not enough to secure the win. The defense knew that there was no way we were going to put the ball in the air, so they played for the run. After our punt, the Raiders had time left for one last drive, but Verlon and company held. Lamonica was forced into throwing a lateral to avoid a sack. Our outside linebacker Ralph Baker alertly recovered the lateral.

The Jets were AFL Champions and I was heading back to Miami to play in Super Bowl III. Jim Hudson, George Sauer, John Elliot, and Pete Lammons were heading back too, except they had better memories of the Orange Bowl than I did. All four were Longhorns and all four loved that field. Especially Pete, who played linebacker for Texas as well as tight end and intercepted me twice only four years earlier.

Clickity clack. The Baltimore Colts were the NFL Champions and their films now ran through the Jets' one-eyed monster. Weeb's successor, Don Shula, was everyone's golden boy. He was just 33, a former player who brought

the Colts back to where they should be—the top. And he did it without Johnny Unitas, who had been nursing a torn tendon in his throwing elbow all season. In his place, Shula had the NFL's MVP Earl Morrall on the roster. Before he came to the Colts, he'd been a backup with the New York Giants. But now, he played like, well, Johnny Unitas. The Colts were 15-1 and had just beaten the Cleveland Browns 34-0 in the NFL championship game.

Conventional wisdom was that the Colts were a "system" team, engineered by an owner with vision (how else do you explain his firing Weeb after a .500 season?) and a genius head coach who was destined for greatness. No one player would make or break them. If there was a breakdown, Shula had such a finely tuned team that he would just put in someone else, and they'd lumber on like Patton's Third Army. And after the NFL's Green Bay Packers had won the first two Super Bowls with little trouble, let's just say the media was not jumping on the Green and White bandwagon.

No one disrespected the Jets more than the leading "authority" on pro football. Jimmy "The Greek" Snyder—a bookmaker who came from Pittsburgh's Three Rivers Area (Steubenville, Ohio)—said:

a) "The Colts have the greatest defensive team in football history, better than the Packers,

b) The Jets won't be able to establish a running game,

c) That without a running game, the Colt pass-rush will be hurrying Namath.

d) The AFL is improving each year but the Jets have a tiger by the tail, and

e) The intangibles like the NFL mystique and Don Shula's coaching…give the Colts the edge."

He did add that, "The Jets have good coaching. Walt Michaels is a great defensive coach and Weeb Ewbank is solid."

Keep in mind that Weeb had already won two NFL championships at this point. And in fact, Shula's team had 15 guys on it that were brought in by

Weeb himself. And these weren't punters and place-kickers. We're talking players like TE John Mackey, WR Jimmy Orr, WR Willie Richardson, and both of their CBs—Jerry Logan and Lenny Lyles—not to mention the great one, Johnny Unitas.

The reason why Jimmy the Greek's statements really ticked me off was that he used them to put us up on the board as 17-point underdogs in the game—this just a day after we beat the Oakland Raiders. In other words, the expert odds were 7 to 1 that the Colts would beat us. If you bet even money, you'd get no points, but a 7-to-1 payoff. The last time there was such a huge underdog in Miami was when a young fighter named Cassius Clay faced Sonny Liston in 1964.

Now football, like life, is a lot about self-confidence. Verlon Biggs knew it. That's why he started the "facial hair club" back when we were 3-2. Since that time, we were 9-1, the only loss coming from the *Heidi* game. But if you hear the same thing over and over again from just about everyone with an opinion, it's only a matter of time before doubts creep in. And we had to sit around for two weeks before we played this game, hearing this same crap over and over again.

The way I looked at it, we were good. We didn't expect to lose. And I'll say it again. We did not expect to lose. So I answered questions sincerely. It may have sounded like I was trying to channel Ali, but I didn't go out of my way to hype anybody up. It was just me being the way I was, giving my honest opinions. All of the words and talk about how good the Colts were, and how we might not have measured up, didn't warm my heart. I didn't need to hype anyone on our team. They didn't need it. They felt good. We knew we were close to a dream coming true. It was an opportunity to do something great, and those kinds of opportunities don't come around every day. It may never be there again. This was it.

Now, Weeb didn't feel the need to speak his mind the same way I did, as he had asked us to keep our mouths shut like good little NFL players, but he didn't stop me from being me.

The first thing I said was that Colt quarterback Earl Morrall, who was the NFL's Player of the Year, would be the sixth best quarterback in the AFL. There was Oakland's Daryl Lamonica, Miami's Bob Griese, San Diego's John Hadl, me, and Vito "Babe" Parilli who were better. In my opinion. I said that to Dave Anderson of the *New York Times* on January 2 on the charter flight down to Miami when asked about my counterpart Earl Morral . A lot of papers picked it up.

On January 3, we were in a players meeting in the morning, and rarely does it get interrupted by anyone, but the Jets business manager, John Free, interrupted the meeting and asked to speak with me a moment. I went outside and he introduced me to two FBI gentlemen. And so we went into a private area and they asked me if I recognized any of the pictures they had. This was the FBI; you don't lie to the FBI. I pointed out a guy who had threatened to shoot me earlier in the season for messing around with his wife (I promise you that was untrue), so I had dismissed his initial threats. However, the same guy was now wanted by the FBI for some other reason, like robbing a bank, and they suspected he was in Miami for the game. They ended up getting him, but it was a focus breaker.

The next night Jim Hudson and I had dinner at a place called Jimmy Fazio's. We ran in to the Colts' place-kicker and short-yardage defensive lineman Lou Michaels. Lou had played with my brother Frank when he was at the University of Kentucky and was the brother of our head defensive coach Walt Michaels.

Lou came with an offensive lineman, Dan Sullivan, who was a starting guard for the Colts. So there was Sullivan and Michaels, and Hudson and me. And when we got together, it was at the bar, and everything was fine until we got into the talk—just talking—and Lou brought up the game.

"You know, we're gonna beat your behinds."

"Oh, come on, Lou, let's not get into that now."

"No, I'll tell you why, Joe."

by Joe Namath

"Yeah, okay, why?"

"Because we got the man to come in and do it."

"You talking about Johnny?"

"Yeah."

"Lou, Johnny's got a bad arm, man, he can't throw the ball across the street." And then with my mischievous sense of humor, I said, "And besides, Lou, what do you know? You're just a kicker."

Ooooh, man, he stood up, his back straightened, and that big square jaw stuck out, and it looked like he was fixing to kill somebody. The maître d' saw Lou get up and jumped in.

"Hey, come on, you guys, we got your table ready," and luckily for me the transition was smooth. We went and sat down and just continued BS-ing. We didn't talk anymore about the game. That was it. Guys should know whenever they get to a certain point.

Lou had an attitude, pushing me, starting up that conversation. He was just having a little fun that nearly got out of hand.

Reports came out that Lou and I had the run-in, especially in the Colts locker room, and by Monday the 6th, Don Shula responded. "I guess Namath can say whatever he wants."

But you know what? Our offensive linemen sure didn't feel that way. They'd joke and all, but they were the ones who had to fight in the pits for the entire game. "Joe, why are you running your mouth? Don't say things! We've got to play against those guys."

All of the "Angry Colts" press increased the betting line even further. We went to 18-point underdogs, eventually 19, because so much money was being laid on Baltimore. Forty-nine of fifty-five writers took the Colts and *Sports Illustrated* had them winning 43-0. We would be lucky to get out of the game alive. No one pointed out that our players were getting angry too.

Weeb kept the films running, focused on strategy. The Colts defense had several defensive formations and a variety of blitzes. But it wasn't that their defensive formations or their blitzes were so good. It was that their players were so good at executing. They were a veteran team. Their average player age was 29.

But they beat teams that were less skilled than we were. The films showed that Colts' opponents were just not as good as our Jets. The Colt defense had never played against an offense like ours. But we were a lot younger and less experienced. Our average age was 25.

Our starting offensive line was hungry, tough, and quick. With four years protecting an 8- to 10-yard quarterback drop under the tutelage of coaches Chuck Knox and Joe Spencer, they had honed the art of pass blocking. Pete Lammons at tight end, Dave Herman at right tackle, Randy Rasmussen at right guard, John Schmitt at center, Bob Talamini at left guard, and Winston Hill at left tackle were one mean fighting machine. There is a reason why I didn't miss a regular season or postseason game for my first five years in the pros. These guys were that reason. Along with Dr. Nicholas.

Now I figured that after watching many hours of the Colts defense on film, I'd get what I saw. The bottom line was that the Colt defense wouldn't adjust for anybody or anything. Are you kidding me? The Colts didn't have to. Would you? After winning the NFL championship game 34-0, you're gonna adjust? For what reason? For who?

Those guys already had their winning shares spent. They joke about it today, but back then, it wasn't so funny. They were already counting on that $15,000 check for the winners' share. How do you prepare a team that's 15-1? How do you fix a team that has nothing wrong with it? That was their attitude. They weren't adjusting anything. They would flat-out beat us at the line of scrimmage, end of story. Even though they may have felt, or someone may have felt, that they should adjust, what were they gonna fix? Well, if you don't change it, something bad is gonna happen. If you do change it, your team says, "Excuse me, why are we changing for these guys?"

The intangible factor was being the underdog—a heavy underdog. Many Jet players had been thrown away by the NFL. They'd been told they were no good, laughed at as second rate. And the NFL franchise that did most of the dumping on Jet players was the Baltimore Colts.

Johnny Sample, our defensive captain, started at cornerback for the Championship Colts in 1959. To say that Johnny had a chip on his shoulder about the NFL was putting it mildly. The title of his autobiography was *Confessions of a Dirty Ballplayer.* Weeb signed Johnny when no one else would.

Don Shula cut offensive lineman Winston Hill in his rookie year after being schooled in practice by veteran defensive lineman Ordell Braase. Weeb picked Winston up for the Jets.

Winston would line up against Braase in the Super Bowl and played possum for reporters:

"It was Braase who was my undoing. I remember when I found out he'd been to war. I thought they were talking about Vietnam. But the man had been in the Korean War."

Our free safety Billy Baird was cut that year too. Shula preferred Jerry Logan. Weeb picked Billy up for the Jets.

Mark Smolinski was one of Weeb's Colt halfbacks. Shula cut him. Weeb picked Mark up for the Jets.

Jets

WEEB EWBANK
Head Coach

11 JIM TURNER
K-QB 6-2 205 27

12 JOE NAMATH
QB 6-2 195 25

13 DON MAYNARD
FL 6-1 179 31

15 BABE PARILLI
QB 6-0 190 38

22 JIM HUDSON
DB 6-2 210 25

23 BILL RADEMACHER
SE 6-1 190 26

24 JOHN SAMPLE
DB 6-1 204 31

26 JIM RICHARDS
DB 6-1 180 21

29 BAKE TURNER
OE 6-1 179 28

30 MARK SMOLINSKI
FB 6-1 215 29

31 BILL MATHIS
HB 6-1 220 29

32 EMERSON BOOZER
HB 5-11 202 25

33 CURLEY JOHNSON
P-TE 6-0 215 33

41 MATT SNELL
FB 6-2 219 27

42 RANDY BEVERLY
DB 5-11 198 24

43 JOHN DOCKERY
DB 6-0 186 23

45 EARL CHRISTY
DB 5-11 195 25

46 BILL BAIRD
DB 5-10 180 29

47 MIKE D'AMATO
DB 6-2 204 25

48 CORNELL GORDON
DB 6-0 187 27

50 CARL McADAMS
DT-LB 6-3 245 24

51 RALPH BAKER
LB 6-3 235 26

52 JOHN SCHMITT
C 6-4 245 24

56 PAUL CRANE
LB-C 6-2 205 24

60 LARRY GRANTHAM
LB 6-0 212 30

61 BOB TALAMINI
OG 6-1 255 29

62 AL ATKINSON
LB 6-2 230 25

63 JOHN NEIDERT
LB 6-2 230 23

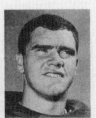

66 RANDY RASMUSSEN
OG 6-2 255 23

67 DAVE HERMAN
OG 6-1 255 27

71 SAM WALTON
OT 6-5 276 25

72 PAUL ROCHESTER
DT 6-2 250 30

74 JEFF RICHARDSON
OT-C 6-3 250 23

75 WINSTON HILL
OT 6-4 280 26

80 JOHN ELLIOTT
DT 6-4 249 23

81 GERRY PHILBIN
DE 6-2 245 27

83 GEORGE SAUER
SE 6-2 195 24

85 STEVE THOMPSON
DE 6-5 240 23

86 VERLON BIGGS
DE 6-4 268 25

87 PETE LAMMONS
TE 6-3 233 24

WALT MICHAELS
Defensive Backfield Coach

CLIVE RUSH
Offensive Coach

JOE SPENCER
Offensive Line Coach

BUDDY RYAN
Defensive Line Coach

GEORGE SAUER, SR.
Director of Player Personnel

JEFF SNEDEKER
Trainer

Colts

DON SHULA
Head Coach

2 TIMMY BROWN
RB 5-11 200 31

15 EARL MORRALL
QB 6-2 206 34

16 JIM WARD
QB 6-2 195 24

19 JOHN UNITAS
QB 6-1 196 35

20 JERRY LOGAN
DB 6-1 190 27

21 RICK VOLK
DB 6-3 195 23

25 ALEX HAWKINS
E-FL 6-1 186 31

26 PRESTON PEARSON
RB 6-1 190 23

27 RAY PERKINS
E 6-0 183 26

28 JIMMY ORR
E-FL 5-11 185 32

32 MIKE CURTIS
LB 6-2 232 24

34 TERRY COLE
RB 6-1 220 22

37 OCIE AUSTIN
DB 6-3 200 21

40 BOB BOYD
DB 5-10 192 30

41 TOM MATTE
RB 6-0 214 29

43 LENNY LYLES
DB 6-2 204 32

45 JERRY HILL
RB 5-11 215 28

47 CHARLES STUKES
DB 6-3 212 23

49 DAVID LEE
K 6-4 215 24

50 BILL CURRY
C 6-2 235 26

52 DICK SZYMANSKI
C 6-3 235 35

53 DENNIS GAUBATZ
LB 6-2 232 28

55 RON PORTER
LB 6-3 232 23

61 CORNELIUS JOHNSON
G 6-2 245 24

 **62** GLENN RESSLER
G 6-3 250 25

 **64** SIDNEY WILLIAMS
LB 6-2 235 26

 **66** DON SHINNICK
LB 6-0 228 33

 **71** DAN SULLIVAN
G 6-3 250 29

 **72** BOB VOGEL
T 6-5 250 26

 **73** SAM BALL
T 6-4 240 24

 **74** BILLY RAY SMITH
DT 6-4 250 33

 **75** JOHN WILLIAMS
G 6-3 256 22

 **76** FRED MILLER
DT 6-3 250 28

 **78** BUBBA SMITH
DE 6-7 295 23

 **79** LOU MICHAELS
DE-K 6-2 250 31

 **81** ORDELL BRAASE
DE 6-4 245 36

 **84** TOM MITCHELL
TE 6-2 235 23

 **85** ROY HILTON
DE 6-6 240 25

 **87** WILLIE RICHARDSON
FL 6-2 198 28

 **88** JOHN MACKEY
TE 6-2 224 26

 BILL ARNSPARGER
Defensive Line Coach

 DICK BIELSKI
Offensive Ends Coach

 DON McCAFFERTY
Offensive Backfield Coach

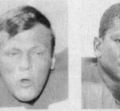 CHUCK NOLL
Defensive Backfield Coach

 JOHN SANDUSKY
Offensive Line Coach

Wide receiver, Bake Turner was a Colt, too. Don Shula cut him for Willie Richardson. Weeb picked Bake up for the Jets.

Curley Johnson spent a year on the Colts taxi squad before getting cut. Al Atkinson was drafted by the Colts, but chose the Jets because we wanted him more. You get the point.

And our leader, Coach Ewbank had his personal reasons too. The "Jolly Green Midget" wasn't getting any respect. Weeb knew every player's skill set better than they did. And the key words he used over and over throughout our pre-game practices were "poise" and "execution."

The way underdogs take the bite out of favorites is by not making errors. Mental errors, interceptions, and fumbles took the AFL out of the first two Super Bowls. We were a confident team, because in our last six games we hadn't hurt ourselves. We hadn't made those silly mental errors, bad interceptions, or lost fumbles.

On the Thursday night before the game, I was invited to the Touchdown Club in Miami to accept an award for the "Outstanding AFL Player of 1968." I was thinking about how the "outstanding player" atmosphere was overshadowing my teammates.

If our defense hadn't played like savages all year... If our offensive line hadn't kept me alive and opened holes for Matt and Boo... If Don Maynard hadn't caught a couple of impossible balls only a week before... If these things hadn't happened, there was no way I would be getting the award.

I got up to the podium, and about the time I'm getting ready to talk, a guy in the back of the room screamed, "Hey Namath, we're gonna kick your—"

I said, "Whoa, wait a minute, I've got news for you. We're gonna win the game, I guarantee ya!" Our team wasn't getting respect and that's how the whole "guarantee" came out. It was not planned, premeditated, it was just anger mixed with confidence.

The next day, a bunch of reporters asked Weeb what he thought of my guarantee.

"That's the way he feels about it, and I'm for him. I wouldn't give a darn for him if he didn't think we could win. I don't think Joe's whistling Dixie at all."

Then Don Shula said, "He's given the players more incentive… Our football team is conscious of everything that goes on, everything that is written. Joe has made it much more interesting."

But Coach Shula's team didn't buy it. With the media and the clippings repeating "the Colts are unbeatable" mantra, they lost their sense of urgency.. When you move into overconfidence, your perspective gets out of whack. You lack the emotional positive of controlled urgency; you lose a beat, a half step, a split second. You're simply not going to perform on your highest level. I knew that because we lost to Buffalo and Denver. I lost the respect for the opponent and that loss was our demise in both of those cases. Were the Colts going to be taught the same lesson?

Well, let me tell you about the coin toss, because it was the only time I've ever felt that way, standing beside Johnny Sample and the official on the sidelines. Just before we walked out there, I started to get a grasp. I knew it was work and all, but I did have time to say, "Wow." And then we started walking to the center of the field, and Johnny Unitas is coming across the other side with Don Shinnick. And I allowed myself to kind of sit back and look at where we were. I felt it. How special it was walking to the middle of the field, Sample and I. There was a vast mix of personalities, fighting one another, like the whole thing had come to a head—Sample, the dirty player, reject from the NFL, and whatever I was perceived to be, and here we were, the captains. Me and the legends and the champs of the great Colts and all that—it was wonderful, and I felt good about it.

SUPERBOWL

Third World Championship Game

Jets vs Colts

AMERICAN FOOTBALL LEAGUE CHAMPION
NEW YORK JETS VERSUS
NATIONAL FOOTBALL LEAGUE CHAMPION
BALTIMORE COLTS
SUNDAY, JANUARY 12, 1969
ORANGE BOWL, MIAMI, FLORIDA

SUNDAY, JANUARY 12, 1969 · 3:00 PM
ORANGE BOWL, MIAMI, FLA. $12.00

21 NA 76 99
ENTER GATE   SECTION   ROW   SEAT

THIRD WORLD CHAMPIONSHIP GAME/JANUARY 12, 1969, ORANGE BOWL, MIAMI, FLORIDA/PRICE $1.00

We got the ball. We threw in something early on to distract their focus. Coach Ewbank wanted to give them a little something extra to think about, so we opened up offensively with an unbalanced line. You see, this game has changed big time in that coaches realize that the more they give players to think about, the less efficient that player will be.

I called Matt Snell's number twice. His first carry went for 3 yards. His second carry went for 9 and a first down. But that second carry also took out the Colts' free safety and expert blitzer, Rick Volk. Matt, broke off left tackle with a good head of steam, and Rick came in low head first and boom, no contest! Volk left the field with a concussion. That was a big blow to their defense right there. Our opening drive stalled at our 40-yard line and we had to punt.

The Colts offense was sharp and drove to our 19-yard line. Our defense then boned up and Colt kicker Lou Michaels came out for a 27-yard field goal attempt. He missed it. We got a break.

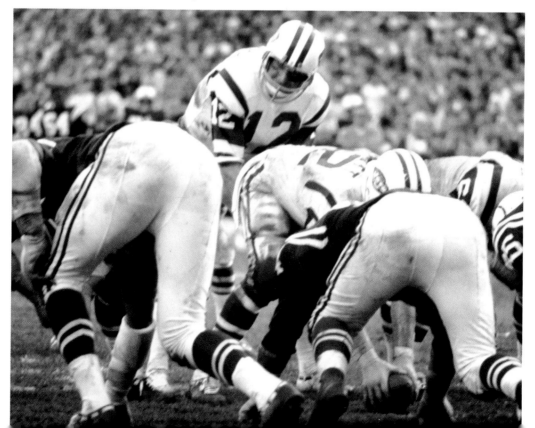

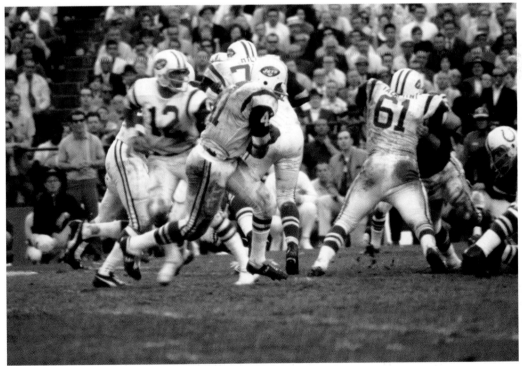

On the next series, our passing game may have influenced the Colt coaches for the rest of the game. I hit Billy Mathis for a 13-yard curl for a first down at our 35. Then, because the Colt defense was playing such good coverage, I went to my last man on the next pass—Don Maynard down the sidelines.

If it wasn't for Bubba Smith, I believe we'd have hit that play. There's a picture of Bubba very high in the air, and if you look closely, I'm falling just a tad off the throw. Bubba's coming at me but I can still focus, I'm searching, I'm tuned into the last area after repetitions of practice. I know its time to do something, and I find Don deep—Don is the last chance I have. It's either throw away or completion.

Bubba influenced that throw, but if Maynard's hamstring was all right, he'd have been gone. Even with the zone defense that had Bobby Boyd and Jerry Logan covering Don under and over, he beat them deep. Now because the Colts played good coverage and our offensive line gave me the time to go to my last read, I went deep. The ball missed Maynard's outstretched hands by mere inches. I really feel that it influenced their secondary for the rest of the day. It had to.

Our possession ended when I overthrew Sauer on a square in route. He was 15 to 17 yards downfield and open. When missed I knew exactly why. I was too pumped. Calm down, Joe.

Our defense held them 3 and out. They had a great punt that put us on our 4 yard line. Matt went off left tackle for 4, then for 5 on a draw play. It was third and 1 and I called an audible. When I came up to the line, I saw that CB Lenny Lyles was laying off George enough to get a quick out over there. And we did. George caught it, and as he turned up field, Lenny hit George and caused a fumble. It's one of those things. They recovered it. On our 12.

The first quarter was over after a 1-yard run by Colt Jerry Hill. Score 0-0. Then Tom Matte goes for seven before Randy Beverly brought him down.

On third and 4, Morrall dropped back to pass. I remember watching our middle linebacker, Al Atkinson, stretch as far as he could as Earl's ball came over his area. He just got his finger on it, and if you look at the film, you see the ball change flight. Al deflected it enough to hit the intended receiver's shoulder pad, tight end Tom Mitchell. The ball bounced way up in the air and Randy Beverly caught it like Roberto Clemente in the end zone for a Jet interception.

The Colts defense was poised. They normally set the tone of the game for that team, and they were holding us to a goose egg. But the interception by Beverly took us from "uh-oh" to "yeah!" They were getting ready to score down there, and Atkinson made just a wonderful play, and we got the ball back. Can you imagine how that lifted us?

Now, the Colts weren't the kind of defense that fooled you. They were the kind of defense that just beat you. They counted on their men beating your men. And why not? Now this game is long past us, so some of us have a tendency to remember the good part, and that's nice. But the fact of the matter is we weren't accomplishing what we knew we could accomplish offensively. And that was because those guys were stopping us and, of course, we were hurting ourselves.

Still, it's an edge if you think you have an idea of where a defense is going and what they will do. But that won't matter if your men get beat at the line of scrimmage. What I remember best about the second quarter is this series. Because of the Colts' tendency to telegraph some of their coverages and the strength of their running defense, we were able to pound what is termed "the weak side." Its success is attributed to our running game blocking on that side behind Winston Hill at tackle and Bob Talamini at guard, with Emerson Boozer and Billy Mathis lead blocking for Matt.

So, instead of calling a play in the huddle, I'd give a formation and tell everyone to "check with me" at the line. What that meant was I would read the defensive alignment, and then call the appropriate play based on the strength of the Colts defense. And if you are trying to beat someone, you attack their weakness. We ran Matt for 1 yard, Matt for 7 yards, Matt for 6 yards, and then Matt on a 12-yard draw play, all directed at the weak side of the Colt defense.

Then, because the Colts began to think, "run," we mixed it up with some passes. Don Shinnick broke up a throw to George, and then on a blitz the next down, I hit Billy Mathis in the flat. But who's out there in coverage? Bubba Smith. He was the consummate pass rusher, but he also had the speed to get out to the flat in pass coverage. He made the tackle on the sideline and held Billy to a 6-yard gain. Just awesome.

We had third and 4. This was our first possession in Colt territory at their 48 yard line. Big down. So, in the huddle, it's a check with me. You go to the line, you see if not what they're gonna do, what they won't do, and you call the play for that anticipated defense.

George catches a quick out that Lenny Lyles almost got to. If it were another couple of inches or so the wrong way, Lenny would have been running in the other direction. But Lenny was so close, but he missed George, who took the ball up-field for 14 yards.

Up until this point, Sauer's been utilized, Mathis has been utilized, Boozer's been utilized, and Don has beaten them deep on an incompletion. I hit Sauer again for 11 more, and then ran Boo for 2. Colt linebacker Dennis Gaubatz is paying more attention to getting out, underneath, toward Maynard, than on covering Snell out of the backfield. So, there was a hole between linebacker Mike Curtis and Gaubatz that Matt could run through. I don't how many times we'd gone to Matt in that situation—it wasn't many—we simply went to Matt because that was the man to go to at the time. I hit Snell for 12.

With first down on their 9-yard line, I didn't even consider the New York cab driver. Matt gains 5 over right tackle. Bubba Smith makes the play.

First and goal from the 9 to get 5 yards is nice. As we huddled up I spotted Lou Michaels coming into the game. In addition to being their kicker Lou was their fifth defensive lineman. He'd come into the game in goal-line/short yardage situations when they wanted to clog up things with an extra lineman. Seeing that he was on his way in, I called Matt over to the weak side again, but told everyone in the huddle to go on the first sound. I was hoping to catch the Colts flatfooted as they had a new defense in and I hadn't gone on a quick count all day. It worked. Matt motored four yards around the left end for the touchdown.

Jim Turner kicked the extra point, and we were up 7-0. I found out later it was the first time an AFL team ever took the lead in a Super Bowl.

Our defense continued to bend a bit, give up some, but boned up when it came to get-down time. Lou Michaels missed another field goal attempt after the Colts drove a little ways down our field. Then we missed one too.

The Colts made it to our 16 on their next possession, when Earl Morrall went for 6 to Willie Richardson who was being covered by Sample. Johnny got some personal revenge. He made his move in front of Richardson and out-hustled him for the ball. His interception put us on our own 2-yard line with only two minutes to kill.

Matt went off tackle for 2 yards. Then again for 3. On third and 5, I called a draw play. Matt was stopped for no game by Bubba Smith. We had to punt twice from our end zone because of offsetting penalties. This put massive pressure on our punter (Curley Johnson, one of the original Titans) as well as our long snapper Paul Crane. But they executed, and with 43 seconds left, the Colts got the ball on our 42-yard line. After a one-yard catch by Jerry Hill, Coach Shula went for the big play.

Colt halfback Tom Matte went into the line with a handoff, then he turned and pitched it back to Morrall. The classic flea-flicker was executed perfectly.

Our defense was momentarily out of position and Morrall had receiver Jimmy Orr wide open in the end zone.

"I never saw Jimmy, I saw [fullback Jerry Hill] in the clear, down the middle," said Morrall. I can understand what Earl was saying. When you turn around in the pocket, you're not necessarily looking at the guy you're gonna throw to. You're "looking off" people. Earl turned around, he saw a receiver wide open down the middle, and he wasn't going to pass him up.

But "layin' in the grass" was our SS Jim Hudson. Hud picked the ball off at our twelve. End of half.

"The play is designed for Orr. Morrall's supposed to look for him," said Shula.

The Colts had five drives end with three interceptions and two missed field goals. Earl Morrall and Lou Michaels must have been the least popular players in the Colt locker room. At least they could sit together. Oh, that's cold-blooded. I didn't say that.

With Morrall's somewhat frustrating performance in the first half, it was only a matter of time before the great one came off the bench.

We kicked off the final half. The Colts took possession on their 25. After a determined 8-yard run, Colt running back Tom Matte fumbled, and our linebacker Ralph Baker recovered on their 33.

We proceeded to burn five minutes off the clock on offense, but had to settle for a field goal from Jim Turner. Jets 10, Colts 0. Curley Johnson kicked the ball back to Baltimore. Our defense held the Colts to three plays and out!

Ten points down with 17:24 to play, a roar went up from the Colt fans. Johnny U. was warming up. If there was an NFL mystique, no one defined it more than Mr. flattop and black shoes himself.

"I'd seen John do so many great things, just watching him warm up—I got scared," this from our head coach Weeb Ewbank. Most everyone knew that one three syllable word stood between the New York Jets and a World Championship… "Unitas."

Man, Mr. Werblin couldn't have asked for a better story. Two quarterbacks, products of the same rugged area. Two leagues. New School. Old School. Challenger gets the ball first.

I knew our defense was playing well, but we had a lot of respect for the Colts offense and believed we needed at least 17 points to win any game. We weren't counting on winning games by scoring 6, 8, 10, or 12. It would be wonderful if we did, but your defense would like to have some points up there on the board too.

Our eight-play drive stalled on Baltimore's 23-yard line. Again we had to settle for a field goal. Jets 13, Colts 0.

When #19 came in for the Colts, he ran Matte for 5. Then he threw to Matte in the flat on second down, but Larry Grantham stuck him for no gain. On third and 5, Johnny put the ball where it had to be for Jimmy Orr, but he dropped it. It took all of one pass for me to know Johnny wasn't 100%. I'd seen Johnny pass the ball for a number of years—he didn't look right. And if you continue to watch the rest of the game, you see the passes did not have Johnny's normal velocity. They were going to the right place, but they were under-thrown. The man was hurt. The Colts had to punt.

Points on the board. Thirteen-nothing means they need two scores to take the lead. So we need another score to make it a three-possession game.

Matt ran for 3 yards. I missed George on second down, but hit him for a big first down on third and 7. Now on the Colts' 49 with a first and 10 preparation paid off. At the line of scrimmage I read blitz. Sauer and I had earlier changed the route in anticipation of this situation. George made his normal move (short post) and then broke outside, leaving Lyles and we picked up 39 yards. First and goal, just inside their ten. Matt ran for 4 as the third quarter ran out.

The fourth quarter began on the Colt 6. We ran Matt twice more, but couldn't get in. Keep in mind we *needed* a three possession lead. Jim Turner came in for a field goal, and with 13:26 left in the game, the Jets led 16-0.

Unitas and the Colts began at their 27. He passed to John Mackey for 5 yards, sent Matte on a 7-yard sweep, passed to Richardson for a first, handed to Matte for 19 off tackle, handed to Hill off right tackle for 12 more, and brought the Colts to the Jet 25 in two minutes and twenty-six seconds. He zigged when our Jet defense expected a zag.

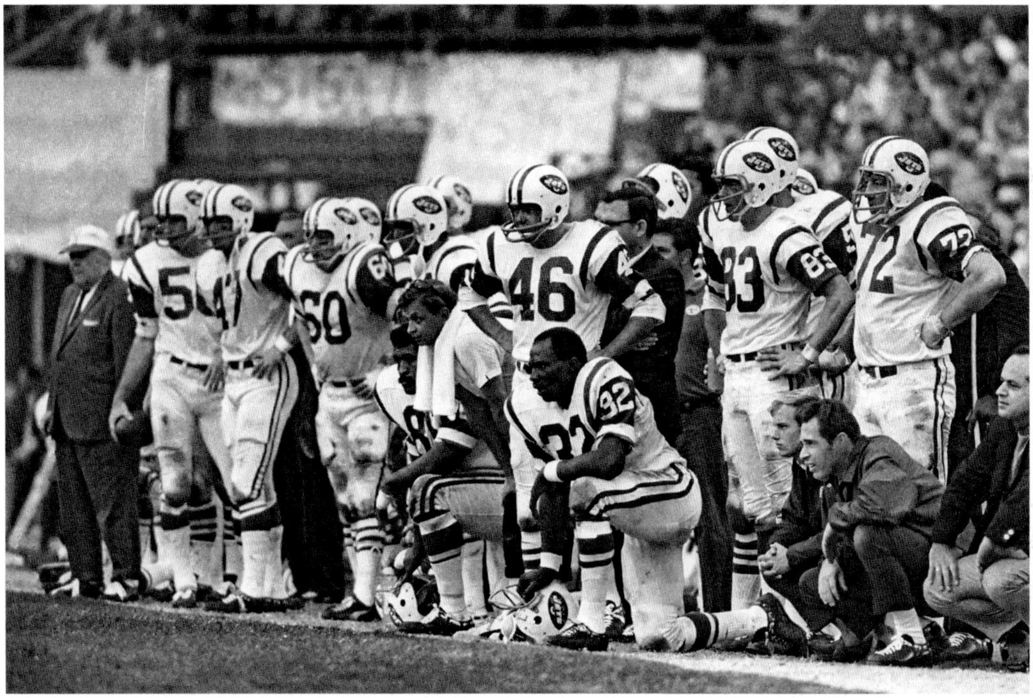

Imagine what he'd have done had he been healthy? But, you've got to remember at this point that we have a three-score lead and our defense is giving up some underneath stuff. Our defense is bending.

From the Jet 25, Johnny U. overthrew Richardson on first and 10 and then went for it all on second down. His pass to Jimmy Orr, though, didn't have the old smoke to it. Randy Beverly stole his second pass of the day in the end zone and we got the ball back on our 20.

The next series belonged to our offensive line and running backs. Snell and Boozer carried the bulk of the load and Billy Mathis added another carry and some excellent blocking. We drove to their 35-yard line, but we missed the field goal. Now only six and a half minutes to play.

Unitas began the next series with three straight incompletions. The king was struggling. But on fourth and 10 with the game on the line, he hit Jimmy Orr for 17 yards. Darn it, we were so close to sealing the game on that fourth and ten. It wasn't over yet.

In three minutes fourteen seconds, Johnny looked like new again as he pushed the Colts down for a touchdown. Jets 16, Colts 7.

With only 3 minutes left and down two scores, Baltimore had no choice but to try an on-side kick. We had our on-side receiving team out there, but the football takes strange bounces. The Colts recovered the kick. With the crowd thundering, Unitas came back on to the field. He hit Richardson for 6. Then Orr for 14. Then Richardson again for 5. The Colts stood on the Jets 19-yard line with a first down and more than two minutes left to play. Some might think that that's not a lot of time, but it can be more than enough time. A touchdown and a field goal would win it for them. And, they already showed that they could recover an on-side kick.

Lead by Coaches Walt Michaels and Buddy Ryan, our defense had been here before. They stopped the Raiders in the AFC championship game. They bent, but they didn't break. Sample and Beverly played Richardson and Orr flawlessly. Perfect throws may have made the difference, but Unitas' magic arm just wasn't healthy. When John's fourth down pass fluttered to the ground, we took possession with 2:21 to play. Our plan now was to milk the clock. Snell, Snell, Snell, Snell—four straight Snells. Delay of game. Snell. Delay of game. Snell. Punt. The Colts got the ball back with eight seconds left but we were the winners.

The AFL and the New York Jets were champions of all football. It was a win for the league, for our fans, for the Jets, and for all the guys who held it together during the early years, and for underdogs everywhere.

There was such a feeling of elation and joy, a tickling explosion inside. It just didn't stop. I still have it! I'm telling you, it still feels that good! I mean, this was a hump to get over, and we did it. Exiting the field, I heard the roar of the crowd. I looked up to them and I raised my arm. I didn't think about it. It was something that came from inside. Number one, yes, number one. We did it.

"How good is Namath?" a reporter asked Johnny Unitas in the locker room after the game.

"Sixteen to seven," Johnny said.

SPORT

DEC. 60¢

02-781

Shakespeare On Quarterbacks:
I Would Give All
My Fame For A Pot
Of Ale And Safety
— King Henry V

Is There A
Future For
Pete Maravich?

The Flyers
Are Ruining
Philadelphia's
Image

He
Jests
At
Scars
That
Never
Felt A
Wound
— Romeo
and Juliet

CHAPTER 08 It's All Right Ma, I'm Only Bleeding

Ya' Gotta Play Hurt

I've always felt sensitive talking about my injuries. With three older brothers, I never wanted to come off like I was complaining. If I complained to them things just got worse.

I started playing professional football with a semi-flat tire after a change in my athletic life that I'd experienced as a senior in college. When you get a bad wheel—after you've been living with the blessings of speed and quickness—it changes things. I was lucky I played quarterback. I couldn't have played any other position after my first knee operation.

When you get hurt, after the initial shock and jolt of pain, which lasts too long, there is a kind of calm that settles over you. And if you're ever to continue playing, you kind of have a better view of the field than a lot of guys who are wondering if they're going to get hurt.

The fact of the matter is that before a game I think most players think about injuries. I knew every game could be my last one. I don't want it to sound morbid. It's just a game. It's not like death. But injury is unavoidable in football.

Standing beside a 6' 7" defensive lineman, a big dude with red eyes and sweat pouring down his face, just waiting to hear introductions before the game, I've thought about it. Yeah, I've thought about it.

You hear people say the game's so much fun somebody would play it even if he weren't being paid. But that doesn't make any sense in the pros. The athletes are so big and fast, the game is too dangerous to play just for the fun of it. Every week one of your friends is limping off the field or getting carried off on a stretcher and that has to make you stop and think. And then there's all the time it takes, the mental strain it puts on you week after week, the pressure it puts on the family life of the married guys. I didn't really appreciate what married guys were going through until I started my own family. I don't know how players and wives of players are able to handle the strain. I mean, you know what the priority is professionally: complete devotion to a team effort. That's fine if you don't have a family around.

But when you do, how do you juggle the priorities when it comes to dealing with the emotional toll it takes on your wife and kids? You can't help but think about your children or your wife and how you're not home and what they're doing. To play pro football effectively, you should have near tunnel vision.

Let's put it this way, if they tried to run the National Football League on fun alone, I don't think they could field one team.

Playing football is also a lot about luck. Some guys are just born to get hurt. No matter how big, strong, fast, smart or careful they are, they just hit the turf the wrong way or fall down weird. And every pro player gets hurt. It's no wonder that the average length of a pro football career is less than four years.

I consider myself one of the lucky ones. When I started, I thought I had maybe four years of professional football in me. I ended up playing 13 seasons. And I never took any of them for granted. But just for "fun," here's a little injury history from my days on the gridiron. I'm not counting bumps, bruises, or my ego.

1952:   Cut lip while playing tackle football in our backyard. Ran into house so mama could love me.

1955:   My first real confusing football pain came when I was 12. I came off the field in Darlington during one of our Little League games and I remember lying on the bench and showing my coach the area that hurt and he said, "Oh, that's... You have groin pains ." And I interpreted that as having growing pains.

I thought, great! I'll be getting taller. But it hurt and I didn't grow a bit.

1960:   I had a pitiful sprained right ankle in our game against Sharon High. Even back then a sprained right ankle was a nagging injury. It seemed to bother Coach Bruno more than it bothered me. As I was also the team's punter, I had to promise Coach Bruno that we wouldn't have to punt against our next opponent. We didn't have to. We beat New Castle 39-0.

I separated my left shoulder on a second down early in the first quarter of our game against Ambridge. I still have the lump. I managed to come back on fourth down and punt. After the game we got on the bus to come home. I went and sat down behind the driver's seat and when my buddy Whitey got on the bus he slammed me square on the shoulder and said, "Good game!" What pain.

At any rate, we went to the hospital and they checked on me and I'd torn something. The doctor at the hospital said, "Season's over." I didn't buy it. Coach Bruno didn't buy it. Because we both said, "Wait a minute, can't be!" There was an orthopedic specialist named Burkeman who was pretty famous locally for operating on Arthur Godfrey.

When we got to Dr. Burkeman's office, we never even sat down. We told him what was up and he just reached over and put his hand on my shoulder.

"Ahh," he said. "Tell you what, we get some foam rubber, we cut out a donut there, just put it over that. That's all right, you'll feel okay." And he was right!

If Doc Burkeman had not given us the okay, life would've been awful. If he says you can't play, should I play? Just because my heart wants to? I wouldn't have. I would have waited, healed, and played baseball. Or I could've ended up in the Blue Room beating cue balls around for the rest of my life. It was Doctor Burkeman's evaluation at that time that kept me moving in my football life.

1961: When I was a freshman at Alabama, I thought I had sprained my right ankle. It hurt but wasn't discolored or swollen. I walked into the training room and overheard a player with a bad arm talking to the trainer.

"Every time I lift my arm up like this it hurts, Coach."

"Well, son, then don't lift your arm up like that! You gotta look the lick in with your head up. We don't arm tackle around here."

I turned right back around and left. I just thought I was hurt.

Spring 1962: We had another day left that the NCAA allowed us to use for practice after our spring game. I was running the same option right play that got me in trouble with Coach Bryant last fall. I executed that pitch perfectly on the option, and then I got hit. Boy, the second I got hit, I knew something was bad. I'd never had a hip pointer before, but they can be debilitating.

I nursed that injury for a couple of months.

1962: The only time that I was in traction in my life, up until the late '80s, also came at Alabama. I was playing right defensive corner (you went both ways back then, because there were strict limits on substitutions), and Marlon Mooningham came running around left end. Now, Marlon was like a bowling ball. He was short, stocky, and powerful. And when I came up to make the play, he lowered his head and I lowered mine as much as I could with my eyes still up and our heads collided. I hurt my neck a little bit and ended up in traction for a few days. Oh, and I lost a back tooth.

1963: Right before the spring game, when I needed to prove myself to get back on the team, I somehow got a heel bruise on my right foot. I had it shot up with painkillers before the game so I could play.

Back then, you believed what the trainers and doctors were telling you. Sure, the injury was painful, but you could play. You had to bite the bullet, or you weren't with the program.

I imagine there still are guys who take injections to play. And guys trying to make the professional football team in August are not going to miss any time on the field to prove themselves. Getting shot up for practice is odd, though.

But under the conditions that I felt? I couldn't even put weight on my heel, it hurt so badly. Take an injection and you can play? It was okay then. You didn't talk about it; you just did it. However, you did have to deal with the pain when the injection wore off. Fun, huh?

1964: In the fourth game of the season, I hurt my right knee against North Carolina State. I was told the first injury was a medial (the outside part of the knee) meniscus cartilage tear, along with a strain of the medial collateral ligament. We knew something was torn because when we aspirated my knee there was blood in the synovial fluid. No one had hit me when I hurt my knee and the general opinion of that kind of injury today is that in all likelihood it's a cartilage tear. That alone can be debilitating. Even with rest, proper care, or repair, it can be career threatening.

Compared to today's medical standards, orthopedic surgery, and knee problems especially, were not all that well analyzed. This was the era of "suck it up" and get back out there. Coach Bryant played with a broken leg. I guess I could suck it up a little bit.

I did more damage to it against Florida in late October, and then by the time we hit the Orange Bowl in late December, the thing was really unstable. I hurt it again in practice and I didn't expect to play.

1965: So when The Jets' orthopedist Dr. James Nicholas, the preeminent guy in his field opened my knee up in January 1965, he found a bit of a mess. It wasn't reported at the time, but the anterior cruciate ligament had been severely torn. The ACL is responsible for basically keeping the knee stable forward and backward, and without one, you have kind of a marionette quality to the joint.

Today, surgeons reconstruct the ACL with grafts from other tendons from the area or from cadaver tissue, but back then, there was nothing Dr. Nicholas could do beyond stapling the ligaments together.

Also the medial collateral ligament, the one that stabilizes the inside of the knee, was torn. Dr. Nicholas stapled it back together so that it held the knee in place as close to straight as possible and he also removed floating cartilage pieces that had a tendency to get caught in the crevices of the joint and painfully grind.

At the end of my rookie year in 1965, I asked Dr. Nicholas to operate on my right knee again. It hurt like heck, and it just wasn't right. The inevitable junk that breaks off during a hard season was grinding in and out of the joint. The team decided not to operate.

1966: In a preseason game against the Houston Oilers at Legion Field in Alabama, my southern home crowd saw me tear up the lateral meniscus of my right knee and the cruciate ligament of my right knee in August. I played that season.

Because my right knee was not being cooperative, I favored it and put most of my weight on my left leg. Throughout 1965 training camp, through the 1965 and 1966 seasons, I had pain in the left knee In December of 1966 Dr. Nicholas diagnosed my left patella tendon as having a case of bursitis (inflammatory swelling of the tendon) due to the additional strain on that leg. As the trainer from Alabama my freshman year would have recommended, the best course of action was not to bend it.

So at the end of the season, Dr. Nicholas cut my right leg open again and removed the lateral cartilage and sewed up the torn cruciate (inside) ligament. He also shifted around some tendons in the back of the right knee to make up for the weakened ACL and to give the knee more stability. This technique would be developed further into the classic ACL reconstruction that is the nuts and bolts of today's orthopedic surgeons. Last but not least, he took out twenty-two pieces of bone that had broken off the femur and tibia from my first two years in the league.

1967: In a preseason game against the Boston Patriots in August, the bursitis in the left knee finally weakened the patella tendon enough to tear a small hole in it. It didn't cause a lack of stability, so I was able to play.

In October, against the Houston Oilers, I threw an interception and fractured my right ankle making a tackle. As the break occurred to a non-weight-bearing bone, I was able to play.

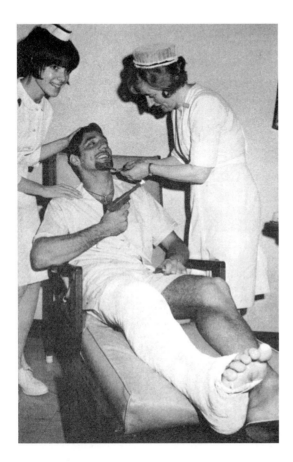

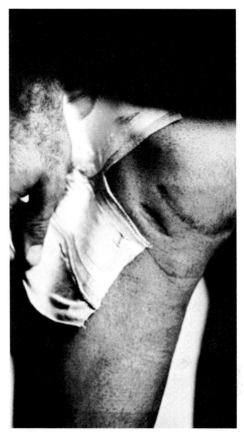

In December, I got a concussion against the Denver Broncos. I think it was the best clean hit I ever took.

It was beautiful. I got rid of the ball to my left intending to hit Bake Turner on a post corner route. Bronco DT Dave Costa got loose up the middle. His head was lowered, and the timing was perfect. Just as I'm letting it go, he connected with his helmet, right smack dab in the middle of my solar plexus.

I bent like a broken twig right over him and his momentum carried me back and jammed me into the ground. The back of my head hit the turf hard, and the initial blow had knocked the wind out of me. Oh, it was awful on the ground. I couldn't catch a breath and my head was pounding.

We took a time out to get me my bearings, but I didn't have to leave the game.

Two weeks later was the game where I broke my cheekbone on a "tough piece of meat" at breakfast and had the minor concussion against Oakland.

1968: I started out the year in an ankle-to-hip cast on my left leg so that the bursitis and tendon tear in my left knee would have time to heal. By March, the tendonitis was no better, so Dr. Nicholas opened up my left knee to take a look.

He found floating meniscus cartilage in the left knee, removed that, and fixed the torn patella tendon. The bursitis has never completely gone away, though. It hasn't till this day. The pain lessened big time, however. I played with it that season and alternated aspirations between the right and left legs, with occasional shots of cortisone (an anti-inflammatory steroid) injected into the joints to reduce the swelling.

In the AFC championship game, I dislocated my left middle finger, and had a minor concussion.

1969: As seasons go, this was a good one for injuries, I guess. I got a scare with my right knee in September against Buffalo, and had a bruised breastbone and concussion against Denver later that month. In other words, nothing really to speak of.

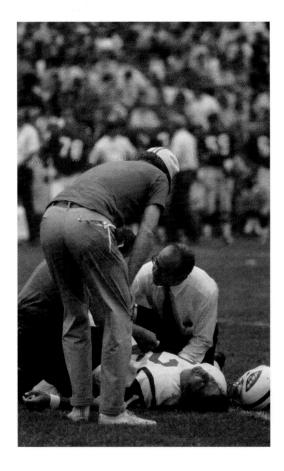

1970: In 1970, the leagues were officially merged, and we joined the
AFC East along with the Baltimore Colts. Looking back now, it
seems the Colts took every opportunity to get even with Joe and
the Jets. In early October 1970, I broke my wrist on my throwing
hand against the Colts at Shea Stadium.

Oh, I remember how I hurt it, too, by the way. Billy Ray Smith, the defensive tackle for the Colts got to me just after I'd thrown a pass. He was driving me back, and the first thing that hit the ground with his weight and mine was my right hand breaking the fall. Problem was I broke my wrist. We still had some time left on the clock, and I ended up throwing a few more passes until the game was over. Every time I threw, it hurt.

After the game, we went to Lenox Hill Hospital and got the official word after the X-rays. The man said to me, "You have a shattered navicular bone." Shattered. That didn't sound good. So we got a cast on, they were keeping me in overnight, and I got a phone call from a buddy named Henry Young, who was an old track guy at Alabama. And he called me and he said, "Hey Joe, don't worry, buddy. Don't worry about this little problem with that navicular. I had a broken navicular."

I said, "Oh yeah?" And he said, "Yeah! I had to keep a cast on for a year, but it healed up, I had no problem at all." Son of a gun, I'm telling you. I had that cast on four and a half months. That's a long time, boy. You know, things could always be worse. I'm not complaining, I'm just saying that was a tough injury.

I had played over five years for the Jets and I had never missed a regular season or playoff game because of injury. That's a fact. After I broke my wrist, my luck turned. I missed the chance to play against the Pittsburgh Steelers, in Pittsburgh, man.

I can remember being on the field and trying to hide my tears. I was out there in street clothes, with that cast on, thinking about stuff, like being home in Pittsburgh and I couldn't play.

And my eyes were watering, I was just trying to hide, you know? I wanted to play, but couldn't.

1971: We were playing a preseason game in Tampa against the Detroit Lions and we had a lead with just under two minutes left in the first half. I wanted to use the clock and run conservative plays so we could end the half and get off the field. I gave the ball to our rookie fullback Lee White for some work. He took it up the middle, and darn if he didn't find a hole and bounced it out to the right outside for a nice gain before he got hit and fumbled. Western PA's own Mike Lucci, the middle linebacker in pursuit of the play, scooped up the fumble and headed toward our end zone. I went to head him off at the pass, to make sure he turned back into the flow of my pursuing teammates. If he gets to the sideline, he's gone.

Oh, I got him to turn back in, but when I got my left arm around his waist, I was flung horizontally into the air kind of like a Frisbee. Then Lion linebacker, Paul Naumoff, while attempting a block, planted his helmet on the outside of my left knee and I was headed back to the OR. The knee isn't designed to bend sideways.

Lying in the trainer's room getting iced down and pampered I thought of my mom. By this time in my career, I could imagine my mother sitting at home, getting word from somebody who had seen the game on television, "Joe got hurt again." And knowing by this time that the actual extent of injuries weren't always reliably reported, I needed to call. I asked John Free, the Jets business manager, to call her to let her know I'd be all right. She knew that Mr. Free was a man that could be trusted.

After the operation at Lenox Hill Hospital My dad and my brothers were there when I came to. Both the cruciate and medial ligaments were torn and what was left of the medial cartilage was taken out.

I found it hard to believe that a knee injury could have been worse than the one I had experienced my senior season at Alabama. But as it turned out, the left knee injury also led to a nerve injury in my left leg, the peroneal nerve. And the most difficult time I had coming back from the knee injury was because of that nerve.

I was lying in my room alone a day after the operation looking down at my leg and feeling like crap. When I went to move my foot, I couldn't move it properly. When I went to wiggle my toes, I couldn't move them. I tried again, and I couldn't move them at all. I got real scared and started reaching for the button to call the nurse or the doctor. Then this little voice whispered to me, "Slow down, Joe. Think. If you have to have something paralyzed, at least it's only your toes." I calmed down some. But I tell you what, I was scared. I couldn't move those toes.

After I buzzed the nurse, she got Dr. Nicholas and we went through a process of figuring out what was wrong. Dr. Nicholas told me, "Joe, I can't tell you whether that nerve was damaged on impact of the injury or whether it was damaged during the operation, but it's damaged." And I said, "Doc, I don't care how it was done, let's just fix it." I knew he was trying to do the right thing for me, and I just wanted it fixed.

Soon after, pain came to my leg and foot big time. The foot would throb, ache and burn. There were times I cried. Before the pain dulled and quieted into a burning numbness, there were electric-like jolts that went from my foot up the side of my leg. Jolts like you get when you grab a hotwire fence like the ones that keep the cows home.

I lost more then 30 lbs. during this time. Before the operation, I weighed 207 lbs., and I was now 177 with a cast on. The shocks would come close to clockwork, day and night, less than every minute, for weeks. It was driving me absolutely nuts. And all they could do for me was give me painkillers.

I can remember the night I went into the bathroom and took a bottle of Percodan and poured them in the commode and said to myself, "This stuff's killing me."

I went out to the stadium the next morning, and Dr. Nicholas and I talked. He sent our trainer Jeff Snedeker out to get a medication called Dilantin. Dilantin is used for epileptic seizures. And when he got back, they put me on a table and gave me the medication and we talked. It got to the point where I felt like they were watching me to see how I was reacting to the medication.

It didn't seem to have any side effects, so Dr. Nicholas kept me on the medication to see if it would dull the nerve. By the next day, I noticed I wasn't getting those jolts as often. They subsided to about every two minutes, then five minutes. The jolts completely stopped in a few days, but my foot continued to ache, tingle, and throb, especially at night.

Now all the nerve guys that Dr. Nicholas and I talked with kept telling us that, "the feeling will come back, we just don't know when." Well, they were right. It came back, but it took

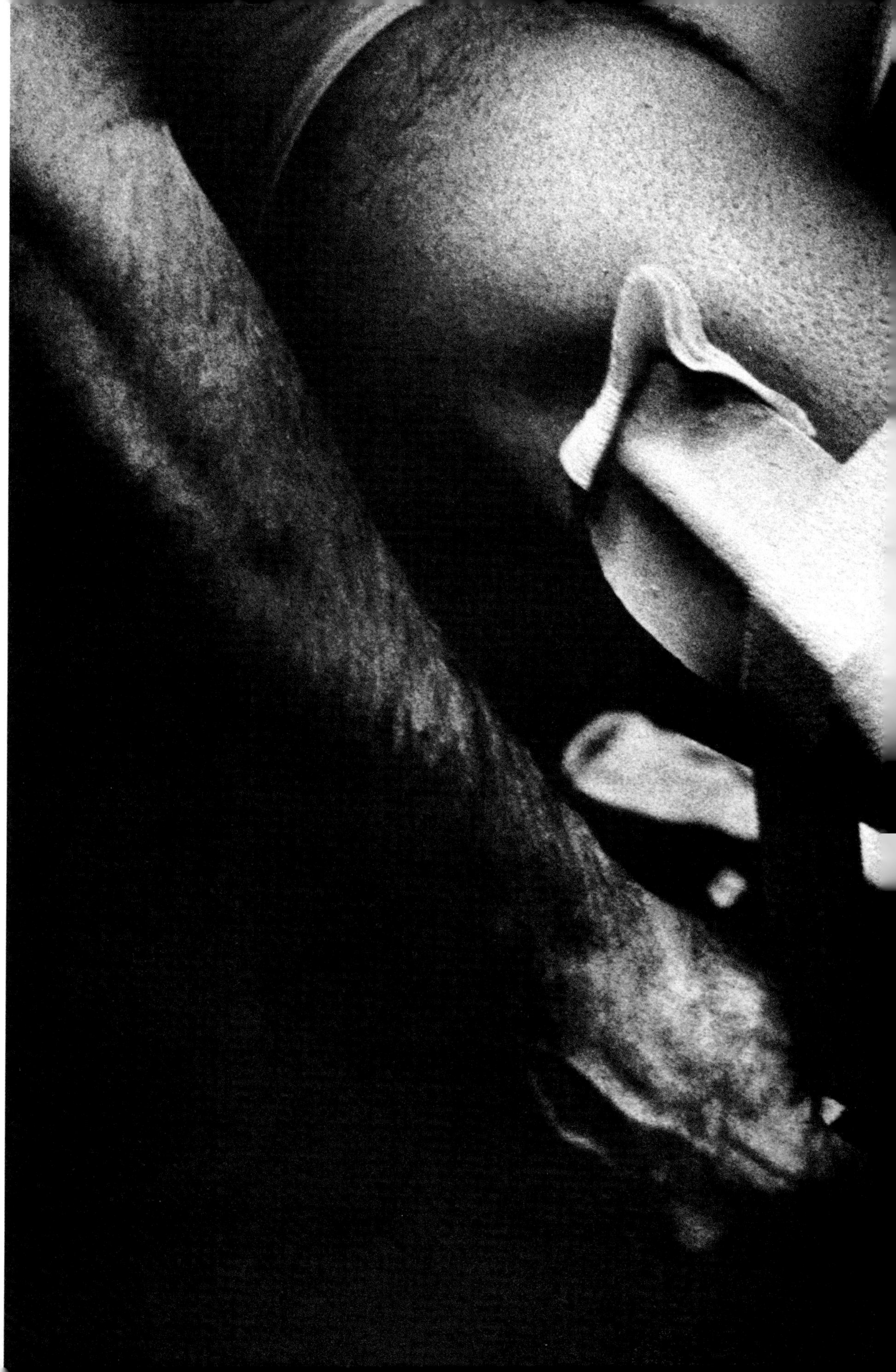

Photo: Harry Benson

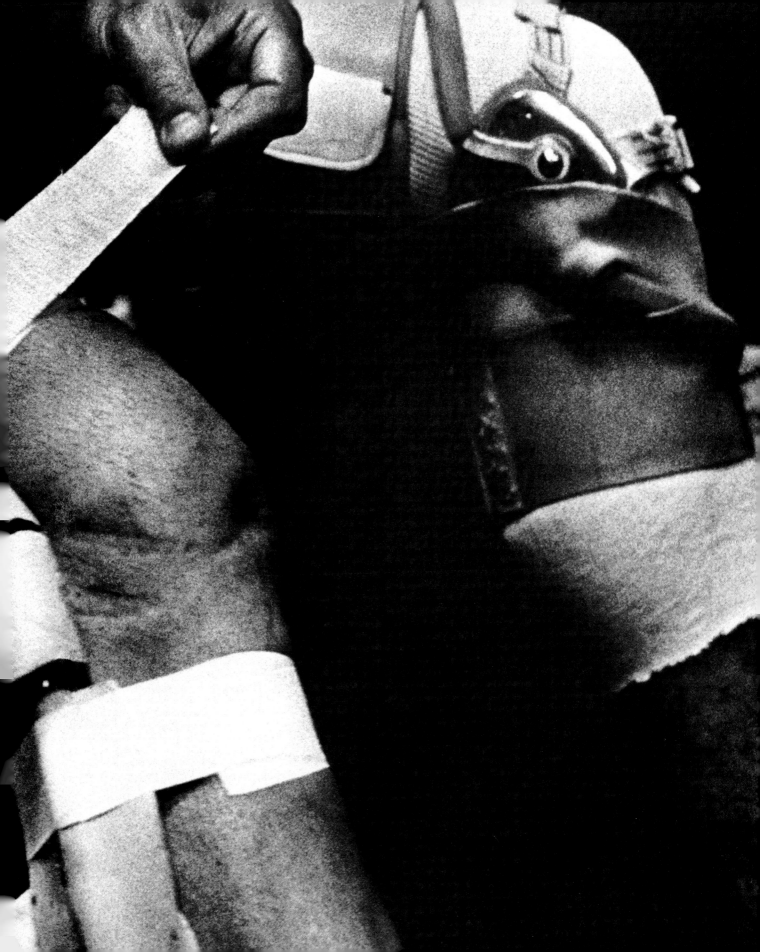

four years and change. Unless you can call numbness and tingling and burning "feeling." I guess you can.

I returned to the field in November. I was so frustrated, so miserable from being hurt—I really wanted to play, and that's the only reason I got back out there. I needed to play, because I sure as heck didn't like where I had been lately.

I got in there just in time for another slight concussion against San Francisco at Shea. We're driving down the field toward the closed end zone. I had just thrown a pass when one of the 49ers was able to deliver a lick to my head and suddenly—gold flash— I'm on the ground. I remember being helped up by John Schmitt, again. I walked over to the 49ers defensive huddle and I put my head in there and said, "Hey, I don't know which one of you so-and-sos did that, but that was a darn good lick." And then I went back to our huddle.

1972: I made it back for an up-and-down year. Twisted my left knee in October against the Oilers, then tore up some lateral ligaments in that pesky right ankle in December, which kept me out of the last game of the year against Cleveland.

1973: Weeb's last year. The Colts again, this time in Baltimore. We have a second down and two at their 3-yard line and I have a bootleg play action pass called. One of our blocking assignments is blown and their middle linebacker, Stan White, comes clean between center and guard. Just as I'm coming off the fake to the running back, he's on me. It was a give-up situation. In fact, I did. When he got to me, I let him take me.

Now instead of falling on my right hand, trying to catch myself and break the fall, I tucked in. The only problem was, like Billy Ray's weight and mine on my hand, all of Stan White's weight and all of my mine landed square on my right shoulder.

And, man, I tore the ligaments. It's technically called the acromioclavicular separation. But most people call them shoulder separations. It felt like my right shoulder was four inches above my left.

I was taken to the locker room and my brother Frank was already there waiting. He called my mother, and then I talked with her. Dr. Nicholas believed that by simply strapping down the shoulder and completely immobilizing it, the torn ligaments would grow back together and heal. We decided not to operate and put any pins in my shoulder for fear of changing my throwing motion.

They put me in a harness, and I stayed in Lenox Hill Hospital for about five or six days. Just lying there. They wanted to monitor me because there was some pain involved, and they also had to continuously tighten the straps that held the ligaments in place. After I rehabbed, I never had a problem with it. I made it back into the lineup eight weeks later.

1974: Freak accident. I went waterskiing with some friends in the off-season and the towrope broke when I was just coming out of the water. As it broke, for some reason or another, I got twisted and my left hamstring snapped.

I had severed two of the three largest muscles in the body in my left leg, and two of them rolled down. Today, what I remember

about this injury is it was the first time I recognized my body actually going into shock. I was in the water and I knew something was wrong with my leg, but I didn't know what. So, as the boat's turning around, I gave the "all fine" signal—I didn't want to panic anyone.

I tell you what, after I was helped into the boat, my body started shaking. I thought, "This is shock." It made sense. You snap two of the three biggest muscles in your body and it gives you an awful feeling of confusion and pain.

I was with a lady friend, and a buddy and his girl, and we went back to the hotel. This was at a resort area in the Berry

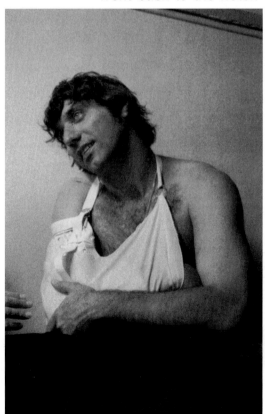

Photos: Harry Benson

Islands, but there wasn't a doctor there. A nurse there had some codeine, and that helped. The famous lawyer F. Lee Bailey was there with his private plane. He would've flown me to New York that night, but the runway didn't have lights, and it was already evening.

So we didn't leave until the next day. They got me to New York, and Dr. Nicholas took a look. He told me they'd never had a successful hamstring reattachment. The case history of a guy in Canada Dr. Nicholas found who did have them reattached successfully in the OR, went through rehab, and tore it again.

Maybe today they have a means of tying up those muscles and holding them up there. Tearing a muscle within itself is bad enough, but when they tear across and are severed, they just roll up or down. Two of the three muscles rolled down the back of my leg. The good news is that the one that stayed attached was the one Dr. Nicholas had used to help give me stability in my left knee.

And when he examined me first, he's examining my knee. And I said, "Doc, no, up here!" and he said, "I know, Joe, I know, but the knee's stable." And he just smiled.

"Okay, so what are we gonna do?"

He said, "There's nothing we're gonna do, Joe. You only need the hamstring to run." And then with that big ol' Greek smile, he said, "You're a quarterback. You don't have to run."

You get through the pain and do your rehab, but in the long run, you can't run. That's what you need your hamstring for, is to run, of course. So, from that time on, the next four seasons were the most frustrating times of my sporting life.

1975: Colts again. In November, I disjointed a vertebra in my neck. A couple of weeks later, I bruised some ribs and twisted my right knee against the Cowboys.

1976: According to injury reports, I pulled what was left of my left hamstring against New England in October. I don't really remember that.

1977: In my final game, I bruised my larynx in Chicago. It was like the Dave Costa hit, except it was a little higher.
T-t-t-that's all folks.

Despite anyone's natural abilities, playing quarterback entails being put in some distracting situations. For example standing in the pocket trying to pay attention to what's going on 40 yards away, meanwhile you hear all the grunting and growling of the beasts trying to crush you. I never cared for that kind of crowd. At the beginning of every preseason, I was always a little edgy back there, a little quick, working my way up to being aggressively calm.

I'm gonna tell you something right here, the first time you get knocked down, it's kind of a shock, but also it wakes you up, brings you back to reality. I can remember the first play I called in college, for the Alabama Crimson Tide. First down, first play of my college career against Georgia, I called the quarterback sneak because I wanted to get hit. That adrenaline was pumping in me, it was so hard, I was so full of nervous energy that I needed to get hit so that I could get into a natural game flow.

After the first hit you get yourself back together, and say you get hit again. The second one is not as bad as the first. And by the time you've been knocked down enough, what difference does the next hit matter? You've got a job to

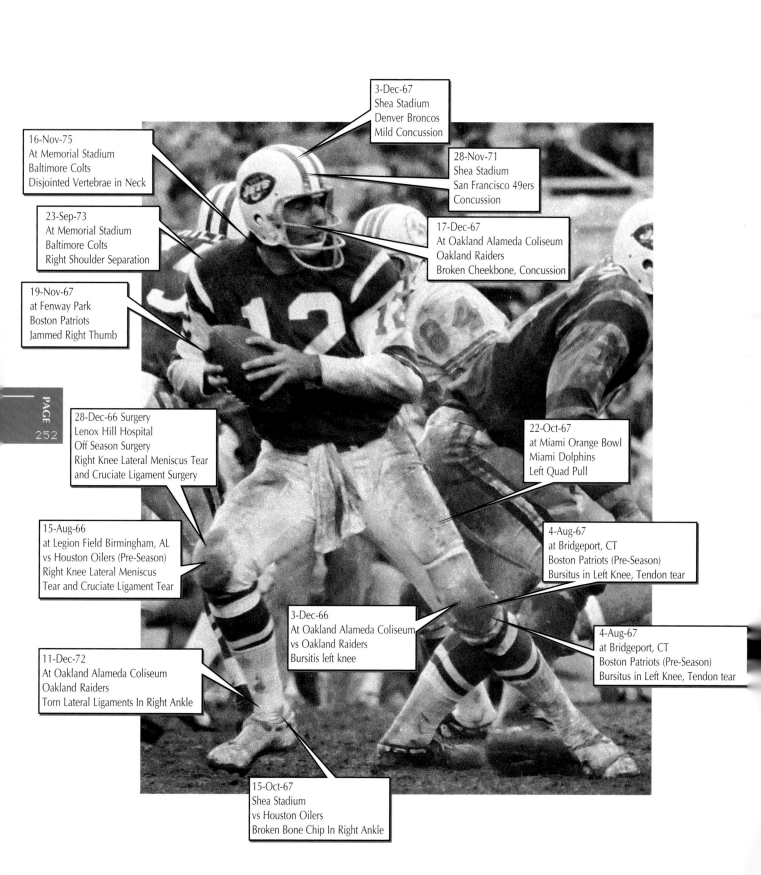

3-Dec-67
Shea Stadium
Denver Broncos
Mild Concussion

16-Nov-75
At Memorial Stadium
Baltimore Colts
Disjointed Vertebrae in Neck

28-Nov-71
Shea Stadium
San Francisco 49ers
Concussion

23-Sep-73
At Memorial Stadium
Baltimore Colts
Right Shoulder Separation

17-Dec-67
At Oakland Alameda Coliseum
Oakland Raiders
Broken Cheekbone, Concussion

19-Nov-67
at Fenway Park
Boston Patriots
Jammed Right Thumb

28-Dec-66 Surgery
Lenox Hill Hospital
Off Season Surgery
Right Knee Lateral Meniscus Tear
and Cruciate Ligament Surgery

22-Oct-67
at Miami Orange Bowl
Miami Dolphins
Left Quad Pull

15-Aug-66
at Legion Field Birmingham, AL
vs Houston Oilers (Pre-Season)
Right Knee Lateral Meniscus
Tear and Cruciate Ligament Tear

4-Aug-67
at Bridgeport, CT
Boston Patriots (Pre-Season)
Bursitus in Left Knee, Tendon tear

3-Dec-66
At Oakland Alameda Coliseum
vs Oakland Raiders
Bursitis left knee

4-Aug-67
at Bridgeport, CT
Boston Patriots (Pre-Season)
Bursitus in Left Knee, Tendon tear

11-Dec-72
At Oakland Alameda Coliseum
Oakland Raiders
Torn Lateral Ligaments In Right Ankle

15-Oct-67
Shea Stadium
vs Houston Oilers
Broken Bone Chip In Right Ankle

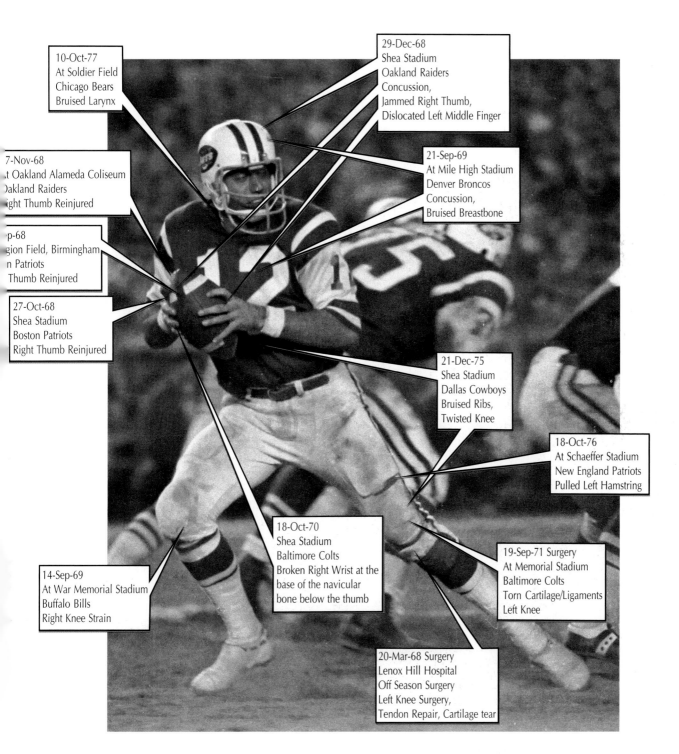

10-Oct-77
At Soldier Field
Chicago Bears
Bruised Larynx

29-Dec-68
Shea Stadium
Oakland Raiders
Concussion,
Jammed Right Thumb,
Dislocated Left Middle Finger

7-Nov-68
t Oakland Alameda Coliseum
akland Raiders
ight Thumb Reinjured

21-Sep-69
At Mile High Stadium
Denver Broncos
Concussion,
Bruised Breastbone

p-68
gion Field, Birmingham
n Patriots
Thumb Reinjured

27-Oct-68
Shea Stadium
Boston Patriots
Right Thumb Reinjured

21-Dec-75
Shea Stadium
Dallas Cowboys
Bruised Ribs,
Twisted Knee

18-Oct-76
At Schaeffer Stadium
New England Patriots
Pulled Left Hamstring

18-Oct-70
Shea Stadium
Baltimore Colts
Broken Right Wrist at the
base of the navicular
bone below the thumb

14-Sep-69
At War Memorial Stadium
Buffalo Bills
Right Knee Strain

19-Sep-71 Surgery
At Memorial Stadium
Baltimore Colts
Torn Cartilage/Ligaments
Left Knee

20-Mar-68 Surgery
Lenox Hill Hospital
Off Season Surgery
Left Knee Surgery,
Tendon Repair, Cartilage tear

do. It gets to where you almost don't notice what's happening to you. I had teammates come up to me after a game and say, "Man, you took a couple of shots out there." And I'd say, "Yeah?" I never cared for bad memories anyway.

Down the line, I knew I was going to have to make some changes. Sure enough when my daughters were born and needed a dad who was physically stable, I decided I had to find a permanent solution for my knee problem. Even though I knew that I'd have to have artificial knee joints (Dr. Nicholas had told me that as early as 1967), being a young fella, I couldn't relate to artificial knees. I thought, "Yeah, sure, okay, someday I'll get them." But now I visualized myself carrying Jessica or Olivia down the steps at an airport or mall, and I could see losing stability and falling while I had one of my girls in my arms. It wasn't like making a big decision. I knew now was the time because I didn't have the stability. It took a lot of hard work to recover from the surgery, but in the long run it has provided me with a lot of relief from physical pain.

Change is one of the few constants that I know of, and I needed to change my life in more ways then one. During my rookie season in '65, I picked up a safety blitz with my left buttock, and after the game every time I sat down it hurt so bad that I went to our number one painkiller: alcohol.

I'll say this about the guys who've played football and are now suffering physically because of it. They were raised and taught, like I was, not to complain and moan about their problems, especially if they are just physical maladies. In my day, the medication was a good stiff drink. And guys like me and those before and after me came to rely in the old stiff drink to get through the tougher times. But I knew this needed to change.

My ex-wife challenged me, told me I had a problem, and having Jessica made me take on the challenge. I made a promise that if I didn't stop drinking, I would check myself into a place and get help. The thought of checking into a dependency clinic terrified me. Getting help terrified me. I didn't believe I needed it. It would be both embarrassing and humiliating to admit that I couldn't stop drinking. So I just quit. And though I was able to stop drinking by myself, I was a dry drunk, as alcoholics call it, for the next thirteen years plus.

But you don't do it alone. And I was never alone in my sober days, because my first sober days, I had my ex-wife and Jessica. And then Olivia came along, so I always had help up until 2000, when we went through the family change. I got stupid or weak or angry, or all of them, and just said, "What the hell," and went back to drinking. And that lasted close to three years.

Now there is not a man or woman alive who has had a drink or two in their lives who has not acted foolishly in front of the opposite sex when they were under the influence. Luckily for me, I just happened to have done it in an interview with Suzy Kolber on *Monday Night Football.*

I say luckily because it gave me the opportunity to see just how far alcohol had taken me askew. I embarrassed my family, friends, fans, the Jets, and myself that evening. While there's no shame in needing help for a variety of things in life, I can't say that I didn't feel shame after that performance. If you've got a brain in your head, you know we all need help from time to time. I learned I needed professional help and was able to get rehabilitation at The Hanley Hazelton Center in West Palm Beach, Florida.

LIFE

BEHIND THE NAMATH AFFAIR

A question of the bad company he keeps

Newsweek

SEPTEMBER 15, 1969

PRO FOOTBALL '69

50c

Namath Of The Jets

FOR TODAY'S MAN

A FAWCETT PUBLICATION   SEPTEMBER 1969

TRUE

60¢

Exclusive:
Namath Tells His Own Story
The Life And Style Of
Broadway Joe

Washington Law Firms:
Where A New Fortas
Scandal May Be Brewing

Rebellious "New" Doctors
Defy The Establishment

Fighting The West's
Killer Forest Fires

Sports Illustrated

Namath Weeps

CHAPTER 09 Lost In The Supermarket

The Selling of Broadway Joe

"I've thought about it more than I've thought about anything so far I've ever done, but it's the only right thing to do. The only right thing to do. And so, I am retiring. I'm finished…" Those were my exact words only a few months after we won the Super Bowl.

At the time, I must have been naïve or ignorant, because I didn't know the extent of what hypocrisy could be until I got into a disagreement with the NFL's rules of conduct over my part ownership of the tavern, Bachelors III. Pete Rozelle, the commissioner of the NFL at the time, told me in June of 1969 that if I didn't give up my interest, I'd be suspended from football. I'd be suspended, he said, because known gamblers had bought meals there and used the pay phones. Mr. Rozelle said those facts were damaging to pro football.

I went through a heavy thought process. I finally decided to retire for one basic reason: I hadn't done anything wrong. I hadn't bet with bookmakers on football games. I'd never lost a game on purpose or tried to shave points. I admit I had deliberately given information to gamblers to affect their bets: I guaranteed that we'd win the Super Bowl and we did. Was the NFL angry?

If that was illegal, I should have been suspended before the game. The whole situation was just filled with hypocrisy. The NFL was filled with associations with gambling. The Hughes Sports Network (Howard Hughes' company) had deals with the NFL while it owned four casinos in Las Vegas. Phil Iselin, the President of the New York Jets, was also the President of a race track, Monmouth Park. The Rooney Family in Pittsburgh owned race tracks, the Mara empire in New York was built on bookmaking, Baltimore's Carroll Rosenbloom admitted on many occasions that he liked to place bets… Some team owners built part, or all, of their fortunes through gambling. There was nothing wrong with that, either.

These owners didn't do anything illegal to get where they were. They were given the benefit of the doubt. Why wasn't I extended the same courtesy? Why did the NFL become so high and mighty since the days in the garage in Canton, Ohio? As long as I did my job on the field, which was a demanding one, why couldn't I own a restaurant?

The real fear was that a quarterback can affect a game with one pass. But instead of coming straight out and saying, "Joe, if you have gamblers eat at your restaurant, it will look like they might be able to influence you to cheat on a game and fix the score," they told me to sell the restaurant or be suspended. If the gamblers owned me already—which they didn't—how would selling my interest in the restaurant solve anything?

It was so obvious to me how ridiculous the NFL's position was that I thought for sure that the media would see the stupidity at play here too. Instead, the consensus was that for the good of the game, I should sell out.

Then the magazines piled on. *Life* was first. They called Bachelors III a "hoodlum-haunted" place. Then *Newsweek*. But *Sports Illustrated* really went for

the cheap shot. They said that I ran crap games in my apartment in January and February of 1969 and that I was just about as dirty as Al Capone. The only problem with their story was that I was in Japan, Okinawa, Hawaii, San Diego and Miami throughout January and February, nowhere near the so-called den of iniquity.

I was feeling lower then a snake's belly. I was sitting in Central Park after playing softball with some buddies, watching all of these people hanging out, playing with their dogs, having a great time. I was just a sad sack, a 26-year-old retiree. And I was thinking, none of these people care about whether I play football or not. Or why. I'm the only one who cares. They don't really care about the line in the sand that I drew with one of our country's biggest institutions—the NFL. Or about how much I was giving up to show how screwed up and hypocritical my profession was. They cared about living in that moment with their family, their dog, enjoying the day. And that made sense to me.

I loved football. It consumed me. I cried when I announced my retirement. I didn't mean to. Seeing those people loving life in the moment made me go back. I needed to play. I missed my people. I missed my game. So I went back.

The NFL was becoming a star system—exactly what Mr. Werblin had predicted—and a star system needs stars to fill the stadiums and seal the TV deals. I would play that role if they wanted me to, and in exchange I would get to play football. Bachelor's III put the cold hard facts on the table. Football wouldn't last forever and there was not the greatest chance at this point that the NFL was going to be extending a helping hand at the end of my career. I remember Don Maynard's line: "It's a cold-blooded business." So, now I separated passion and business and planned for my financial future.

What I did know is that after the guarantee and Bachelor's III, there weren't many people who followed professional sports who didn't have an opinion about me. Some good, some bad, but I think a lot of people knew who played quarterback for the New York Jets.

Now back then, professional athletes were not a big draw for advertising or endorsement contracts. In fact the whole concept of "endorsement" was kind of alien in the early '60s. The most successful ad from that time featured Mickey Mantle, Wilt Chamberlain, Don Meredith, Johnny Unitas, and Oscar Robinson crying, "I Want My Maypo!" It was all about getting kids to push their moms and dads to buy the cereal because their heroes ate it. It worked. And soon advertisers began to open up to the idea that maybe athletes could sell products to people other than just kids.

When I started playing pro ball, I didn't really rack my brain looking for endorsement money. I needed to learn the playbook. So the first advertising dollars I earned were for the usual things—men's clothes, athletic shoes, and soft drinks. What was cool about doing them is that the advertisers found that when they pushed my bachelor "lifestyle" in the copy, they ended up increasing sales. Of course, I did have somewhat of a reputation for having fun, enjoying the wee hours and entertaining lovely women.

There really aren't major inaccuracies about my lifestyle back in those days. I had a lot of fun and I enjoyed what the city had to offer. Weeb had a great theory that it was best to practice at around the same time that we played our ball games. So this meant that we practiced around one o'clock and

This man works only two hours a week.

And his game is a game
But you have to be Joe Namath
for a set-up like that. With his
natural vitality, Joe's leisure
clothes get quite a work-out
Which is why he wears
Wear-Dated' No-Iron slacks. They
hold their crease through countless
washings and wearings. They're
tough enough to be guaranteed
for one full year of normal wear.
garment replaced or money
refunded by Chemstrand.

These Joe Namath
slacks by Liberty are
No-Iron corduroy—
a blend of 50%
Blue "C" polyester
and 50% cotton
in antelope, olive,
navy, light blue.
Men's Ivy League
in sizes 27 to 40, $9.
Regular boys'
Ivy League— slim,
husky, prep, $8.

Joe Namath Scores in Pumas.

On or off the field Joe Namath appreciates the comfort and support of Puma's
full line of leisure and football shoes. Like the comfortable Joe Namath shoe
shown here. All available at your sporting goods store or shoe store or write
Sports Beconta, Inc., 50 Executive Blvd., Elmsford, N.Y. 10523. Or 340 Oys-
ter Pt. Blvd., So. San Francisco, Calif. 94080.

PUMA from Beconta.

44

BOYS' LIFE ■ S

sometimes four o'clock in the afternoon. And as any red-blooded young American will attest, you don't need more than about eight hours sleep when you're vital. So, I could reasonably return home at around 2 or even 3 a.m. and still get enough shut-eye and make it to work ready to go. And if you can't figure out what you're doing by 2 or 3 in the morning, you have a lot more problems than getting enough sleep.

Jimmy Breslin once wrote a story about the night before the AFC championship game. He said that the night before the game I was spotted entering the Summit Hotel on Lexington Avenue in the wee hours of the morning in the company of a young lady. And that I was again spotted exiting the Summit a few hours before kick-off coming out of the hotel wearing my fur coat.

The story was just plain ridiculous. I didn't wear a fur coat that day.

After the Super Bowl, there was a lot of demand for Joe Willie to pitch for their products.

Braniff Airlines asked me to do a commercial with the famous tagline: "When You've Got it—Flaunt it!" Rex International signed me up to endorse a

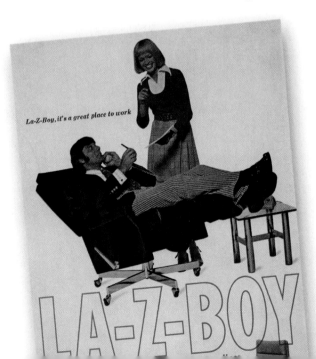

La-Z-Boy, it's a great place to work

"I'm shy with girls. But I kind of like the one who gave me this Solid State Schick Retractable."

Schick's super gift combination!
A free Lady Schick Caprice razor comes with every men's Schick Retractable!

Take a cue from Joe's girl. Give the world's premium razor—and get an elegant Lady Schick as a beautiful bonus!

The Solid State Schick Retractable has an exclusive retractable shaving head. So it's completely self-protected.

The motor is solid state controlled. And the built-in transformer on the Solid State Cordless

Joe Namath is an Olivetti girl.

If you don't believe it
in that Ol

The Bootman.
He's no ordinary
Joe.

Boots are his thing.
They're part of his image.
He knows just how to wear boots.
With style.
He knows when to wear them too.
Whenever he feels like it.
But don't try to con
The Bootman into a boot made
by a shoemaker.
His boots are real.
The label inside all of them
reads "Dingo."
If you don't
believe us, ask
any girl Joe
Namath knows.

dingo

For store nearest you, write: Acme Boot Co., Inc., Dept. PL30,
Clarksville, Tenn. 37040. A subsidiary of Northwest Industries, Inc.
FROM ACME Ⓐ THE WORLD'S LARGEST BOOTMAKER

line of shirts with my name on the label. La-Z-Boy recliners featured me in a series of print ads and commercials. Dingo Boots brought me in as the new "Dingo Man. He's no ordinary Joe." Royal Pub Cologne pitched me as one of its clients: "The kind of guy who uses it, doesn't need it." Puma sneakers gave me my own model of shoe and called it "Swinger."

Noxzema Shaving Cream then got in the act and brought in beautiful women to star alongside me. The first add featured a very sexy actress named Gunilla Knutson who would say with a wonderful Swedish accent, "Take it off, Joe… Take it all off." Then Farrah Fawcett came in for the next one and just about stole the show. My favorite line was, "I'm so excited, I'm gonna get creamed." Then Farrah rubbed shaving cream on my face.

I did work for Olivetti Typewriters, too. The Great George Lois, of the "I Want My Maypo" fame, asked me if I knew how to type. Who did he think he was talking to here? Of course I knew how! I took two years of it at Beaver Falls High School. So George had me act as the secretary to a hard-driving female executive. George changed the stereotypes of the time and at the end the "boss" lady is so impressed with my typing that she asks me out on a date.

Why don't you get into something comfortable?

Then Ovaltine asked me to work with them and do some commercials. They figured if I said that Ovaltine was the right drink for little kids, then they'd just have to have it. So the "Any friend of Ovaltine is a friend of mine" campaign began, and Ovaltine sales increased dramatically. I'd end each commercial with the tagline, "My old pal, Ovaltine."

The Hamilton Beach Butter-Up Corn Popper was my signature product. It was a very good popcorn maker and I love popcorn. We tried to expand the empire with Joe Namath's "Little Mac" Burger Machine, but it didn't do as well as the popcorn maker. I think George Foreman bought the entire unused inventory and called it the George Foreman grill. The rest is history.

For footballs and straight jersey licensing, we did a deal with Franklin Sporting Goods. After the Rex International contract expired, we worked with Arrow Shirts and developed a whole line of Joe Namath sportswear. My friend Johnny Carson was so taken with the idea that he ended up with his own line of clothes too. I hear Donald Trump has one now. And of course, I just had to sponsor bed sheets, so Fieldcrest Mills came up with Joe Namath "The Playmaker Collection" to fill in that gap. The pillowcases had my picture on them. Nice.

And then came one of the most fun ads I ever did. At first I thought Jimmy Walsh was nuts and I never really did like the way I looked or sounded in the thing, but it became the one commercial that people always ask me about.

It was for Beautymist pantyhose. I wore them with green satin shorts and a Jet jersey. The camera panned slowly from my feet up my legs to my face and I said, "Now I don't wear pantyhose, but if Beautymist can make *these* legs look beautiful, imagine what they'll do for yours."

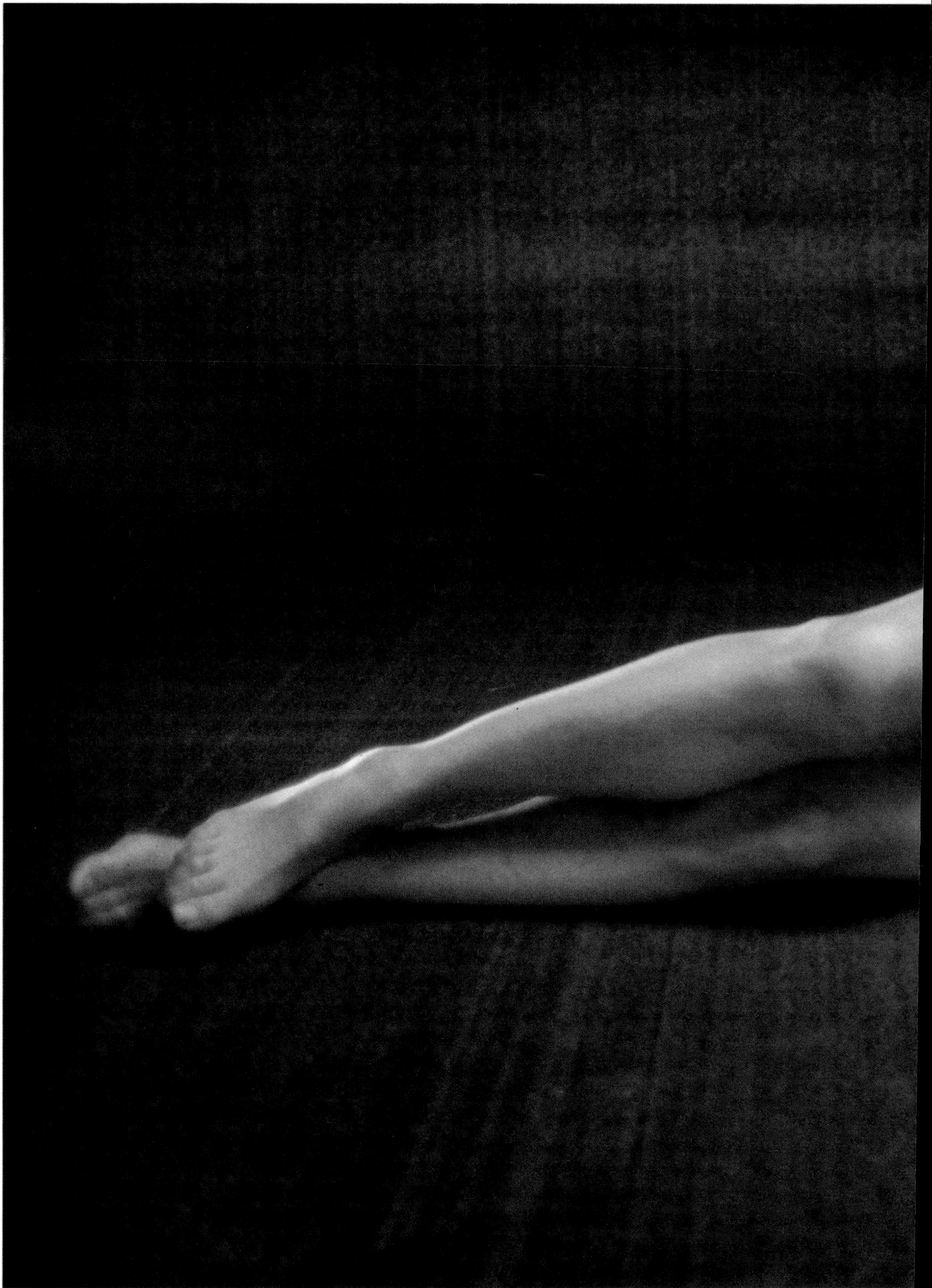

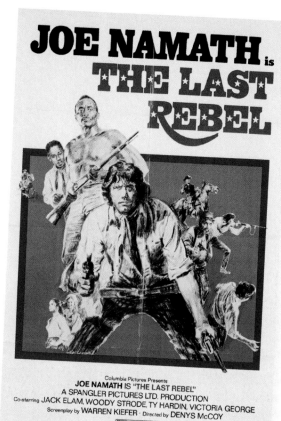

After the Super Bowl, I also started appearing in movies. My first job was a supporting part in a movie called *Norwood,* which starred Glen Campbell. Then, I did a movie with Ann-Margret called *C.C. and Company.* Working with Ann wasn't as much fun as I would have liked to have had, because she was married. Her husband Robert Smith and she are together to this day. After *C.C and Company,* I did a spaghetti western in Italy with Jack Elam and Woody Strode called *The Last Rebel.* I just can't get myself to watch any of those movies today. I was just winging it, doing what I was told. I was a football player and accustomed to getting coached. Wrong.

I could never take my work as an actor seriously because I never developed a passion for the art. I was Joe from Beaver Falls, presented with some opportunities. I was filling roles that I was offered, not because I had a passion to be an actor, or a desire to be an actor, but because the work was so good, I had to see what it was about. And only when I started performing in the theater did I really start to get a feel for acting and an appreciation for the art.

The toughest emotion I had dealt with was going from a level of expertise as a ball player, where I was confident and I had legitimately performed well, to being the star of a theatrical production where I was the least experienced actor on stage. It felt like crap. I knew I didn't know my stuff, everyone else knew I didn't know it, but we had to work together and sell it. I was dealing with an ongoing excruciatingly emotional drama.

What I do know is to be good in any profession, any art, you need a passion. And I never had a passion for acting. It was never a driving force in my life, but rather an opportunity to help get to a position of financial solidity.

Growing up where I did, everything was always, "Money doesn't grow on trees… We're all working." Well, I wanted to get to a place where I owned most of my own time.

CHAPTER 10 | The Right Profile

by James C. Walsh

Joe, Inc.

It is 1963, I've just graduated from the University of Alabama and I don't want to go to Vietnam. Dead or wounded in a rice paddy is not my idea of an attractive future. So I'm about to go into my first year of law school at Alabama and I'm flat broke. I've scrounged up enough money to buy an old Buick and figure I'll drive down to Tuscaloosa and maybe sell it to someone down there. Get my money back and get a free trip back to school to boot. Of course the car breaks down two exits from my hometown exit on the Jersey Turnpike (dear old Exit 9). Stuck in New Brunswick, maybe for the rest of my life.

My sister takes pity on me and gives me enough money to get a plane ticket to Alabama. I have to get there the next day to register for class.

More problems, though, because the plane is going to land in Birmingham; that's 60 miles from Tuscaloosa. How do I get to Tuscaloosa when the plane lands at 3:00 a.m.? I call a couple close friends of mine down there and reach one buddy who says his father won't let him take the car, and this other guy

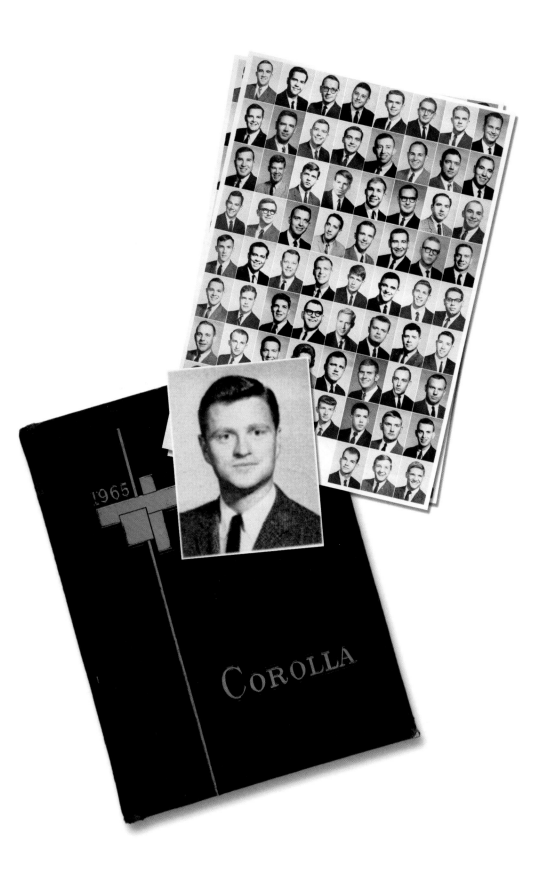

says, "Love to help you, Jimmy, but I got other stuff to do," which is of course code for the fact that he has a hot date. I'm going to be stuck when I get to Birmingham. Sixty miles is better than 1,200, but I have to get to school by 10 a.m. or it's hello, Saigon. Unbeknownst to me, one of my "friends" that I spoke to goes to dinner that night and sees Joe Namath. He tells Joe, "Hey, Jimmy's coming in—wanted me to pick him up, but I can't make it."

You know, all these friends at home and in Alabama that were supposedly close buddies of mine, they all disappointed me. My father drives me to the bus station and I get the bus into Newark Airport. I get on the plane, land in Birmingham and as I'm getting out of my seat I'm really down. I'm really depressed over this—the fact that all the guys who I thought were going to help me weren't going to show. And how do I get to Tuscaloosa at 3 a.m.?

I get off the plane, and in those days they didn't have a Jet way, you walked downstairs onto the tarmac. And as I'm going down the stairs with my head down, I hear this yell. And I look up and there's Joe Namath. It's 3:00 in the morning. The son of a gun has come out in the middle of the night, which is a complete violation of the football team's curfew. He has this buddy of his from Pennsylvania that has driven down there, a guy named Wibby Glover, and he asked Wibby to meet him on a corner after he snuck out of the Bear Bryant Hall, for God's sake, to pick me up.

I first met Joe when my friend and one of Joe's teammates, Ray Abruzzese, introduced us at a pool hall. I thought he was cocky, with his peak billed beret and sharp stick. A bunch of us went on spring break together my senior year, though, and Joe and I went out for coffee at one point in the trip. I learned that Joe was Hungarian. And I am too, on my mother's side. I even learned to speak Hungarian from my grandmother when I was a child. The common blood helped us strike up an early and solid friendship.

We'd shoot some pool together, hang out at the coffee shop, and often we saw each other at Sunday mass. I know that sounds corny, but we were a couple of the few Catholics at Alabama at the time. And Tuscaloosa, Alabama in the early '60s was still the home of the grand dragon of the Ku Klux Klan. In my part-time job, as a bellhop at the Stafford Hotel in downtown Tuscaloosa, I observed Robert Shelton first hand, the Grand Dragon himself, meeting daily with his cronies in the hotel lobby. It was not so long before that the Klan had terrorized Catholics with cross burnings for their support of integration.

After he picked me up at the airport when everyone else had let me down, I knew I could count on Joe. Knowing Joe like I know him now, it makes sense that he picked me up. Joe and I are about as different at first glance as you could imagine. I think what brought us together was the fact that we were both "outsiders." He came from a blue-collar work ethic and busted his chops to get himself ahead. I did the same thing. When my "friend" was dining out on the story about me being stuck in Birmingham to the star quarterback of the football team to impress his date, I think the star quarterback thought to himself, "That could have been me."

Being a close friend of the star QB at Alabama gave me special currency among my law school peers. And being an easterner at Alabama in the '60s made you a member of a rarefied, select group. We all knew or knew of each other. It was a bonding for social survival type of thing. Joe was "adopted" by three widowed and retired schoolteachers, who made Joe and his friends feel at home. They were devoted Alabama football fans and adored the Pennsylvania QB. Three sisters, Bessie Asbury, Ruth Birchfield and Mary Kraut, became our lasting dear friends. We were privileged to attend Bessie's 100th birthday party on December 24, 2004.

In the movie *Forrest Gump*, written by one of Joe's classmates, Winston Groom, there is a scene where Forrest is there when Governor Wallace stands in the doorway and refuses entry to two black students. Joe and I actually watched that happen. Joe's girlfriend lived in the same dorm as Vivian Malone, one of the students refused admittance. I remember U.S. Attorney Nicholas Katzenbach telling Wallace, "You gotta be kidding, Governor, step aside."

Interestingly, several years later, Joe and I attended an Alabama game as the guests of Jets owner Sonny Werblin and Coach Bear Bryant. Governor Wallace was in a wheelchair when the homecoming queen stooped to accept his kiss of congratulations at halftime. The queen was a young black woman. We watched Alabama grow up with us.

I had nothing to do with Joe's record contract, the $400,000 plus deal. I was finishing law school at the time, and Joe put that together with Mike Bite. Don't let Joe kid you, every business deal that involves him begins and ends with him. He was never a "do whatever" kind of guy, like some guys I've worked with before. And he was never a quick buck kind of guy either. It didn't matter how much money was involved or how little. If Joe didn't think you or your company was on the up-and-up, or if he had any quirky inside feelings about the terms, he wouldn't do the deal. Still won't.

Once, Bill Mathis, Joe's teammate, arranged for Joe to get a ski lodge condominium for an appearance at a cocktail party in New Jersey. So Joe, Bill, Bob Skaff and I trekked over the George Washington Bridge in Bill's rented limo. When we got there, Joe decided it wasn't right and decided not to go in. He was adamant. It just didn't feel right to him, so we got back in the limo and headed back to New York. Poor Bill. Talk about being down. He was also getting a condo as his fee for arranging the appearance. To make matters worse, the limo broke down on the way back home right in the middle of the bridge.

Anyway, like many guys from New Jersey, my goal was always to make it in New York. I had just passed the bar exam and I was working as a clerk in the office of a lawyer by the name of Dominic Porto. I had a little desk outside of his office at 274 Madison Avenue, and I was just trying to scrape a living together. Joe and our buddy Ray Abruzzese were playing on the Jets, and they had a great bachelor pad to play cards and hang out in. Their third roommate was horseracing writer Joe Hirsch, who was on the racing circuit most of the year. So I stayed with them when I first moved to New York.

While I studied to pass the New York Bar I was out at night with one of the most famous celebrities in New York. Everyone wanted to know Joe. Welcome mats were always out at the hottest bars and restaurants on the East Side for Joe and his retinue. Being a close friend of Joe's made me a part of the clique.

Early in the Jets' Super Bowl season, I went to one of the games with Joe, and on the way back, he told me that Milton Woodard, who was the commissioner of the AFL, had just passed a rule that players had to shave their facial hair. Joe had grown this big Fu Manchu moustache, and the league said that it was unsportsmanlike or something. So Joe said, "Why don't you see if you can get me a commercial?"

So I called this press agent I knew by the name of Eddie Jaffe. He was an old-time PR guy. Press agents were guys who made a living feeding information to the gossip columnists. The old-timers knew how to get paid from both ends. They might have a restaurant as a client and at the same time have an aspiring young star on retainer. The would-be star's name in Walter Winchell's or Ed Sullivan's column seated near a real celebrity whose visit would be tipped to the press agent was valuable. All the suburbanites who read the New York gossip columns wanted to go to the restaurants the celebrities visited, and the would-be celebrity would gain pseudo fame from the mention.

By this time, I had met a bunch of people directly or indirectly with Joe. At that time, being associated with him as a young, fledgling lawyer was like having a Harvard degree and meeting just about everyone you could imagine who would be able to help you later on in life. But these weren't Harvard guys; they were nightclub guys from all walks of life. There was a whole coterie of people who were old school and knew just about everyone. Some went back to the days of Texas Guinan, of Prohibition fame. Some were old-time PR guys who lived on 48th Street, Joe Russell, Eddie Jaffe, Irving Zussman, Sam Gutwirth, Irving Hoffman, all these characters—really old-fashioned, like Sidney Falco in *Sweet Smell of Success*. And there was a young guy who was the connection to all of them, a fellow named Tad Dowd. Tad Dowd was this great Damon Runyon character, who looks like an Irish guy from Jersey, even though he has the Greenwich, Connecticut, name.

Tad had a bottom-line sense of reality, which earned him the sobriquet, "the truth merchant." Once, when I was annoyed at Joe for keeping advertising guru George Lois waiting for a commercial shoot (Joe had other priorities at the time), Tad reminded me that my responsibility was to protect Joe, and that the ad guys wouldn't give me the time of day if it weren't for Joe.

So Tad and I became great buddies. He was friends with Joe and Ray and Bobby Van, jockey Bill Hartack, singer Tom Jones and all the nightclub guys, and through him I met the legendary Jaffe.

So I make the cold call, like I'm a seasoned veteran. "Eddie, I want Joe to do a commercial." So Eddie, I don't know who he called, but he called some people he knew at ad agencies, and said, "Okay, we've got Schick Electric; they want to do a commercial with Joe." Now I had to get a deal done with Schick that would impress Joe. He was my friend, but he was a shrewd business guy too. If I had come back with a bad deal, he would have turned it down, and his Jimmy Walsh-as-business-partner experiment would have been over. He'd still be my friend, but he would look elsewhere for someone to field and cut his deals. Joe somehow knew exactly how valuable he was, and I wasn't about to sell him short.

After a lot of—let's call it cordial—give and take, I got Schick to agree to the unheard-of price of $10,000 ($120,000 in today's money) for three airings of Joe shaving his moustache. Now Joe came up with the idea, it was his suggestion, no question about it. But I wouldn't agree to a standard 30-second spot. It was three uses. They could only use it three times, first on Ed Sullivan's show on CBS, then once on ABC and once on NBC. At the time, it was an enormous publicity stunt for which Joe was paid handsomely.

So Joe had to shave his moustache with an electric razor. It was a big, long moustache, and electric razor technology wasn't very good back then. So it was an excruciating thing, watching Joe ripping out those hairs on his face with that primitive device and acting like it didn't hurt. By then, Joe was a veteran of living with pain, but this was a whole new dimension. And of course it was one take; there was no going back. He shaves the moustache and that's it. He was so great in it, and thanks to the arbitrary Milton Woodard dictate, Joe was able to capitalize financially and enjoy a great publicity coup. Soon after that, I think, Joe was asked about the hair thing in pro sports, and he said something brilliant like, "The greatest man who ever walked the earth had long hair and a beard. I suppose they'd ask our Lord to shave and cut his hair too." Schick came back and said that it was so successful they wanted to run it more. And then we negotiated again from there and ended up clearing about $30,000 (which is like $360,000 in today's money) from that one bit of PR. The press was worth a fortune—Joe was front page in all of the papers.

Now, I'm a law clerk… I'm sitting at this little table outside this guy's office after this thing goes through the roof. All of a sudden the Jets are going to the playoffs, the Jets win the playoffs and the Jets are going to the Super Bowl. My phone starts ringing off the hook for Joe business. Porto can't mask his annoyance that his clerk is getting all of these important phone calls—movie studios and ad agencies, and all these major companies, wanting to know about how to do a deal with Joe because they just talked to the agency that did the shaving ad and they said to talk to Jimmy Walsh.

I mean, Porto was doing me a favor just by letting me sit there and do something. I didn't know anything. I was a novice. So anyhow, now all of a sudden these deals start coming in.

I'm like 27, 28 at the time, one paycheck away from going back to New Brunswick. Now the Jets are going to the Super Bowl, and Joe guarantees the Super Bowl win. I'm thinking, "I don't know much about football, but if this guy pulls it off, all bets are off." The Jets win and New York goes just nuts. Joe is bigger than the Beatles. At city hall, Mayor Lindsay, who was real popular back then, gets shouted off the stage when they salute the Jets. Everyone wants a piece of Joe Namath, and I'm thinking that if I can convince Joe that I can be the guy to divvy up the pieces, he'll never have to worry about money or providing for his family again. But one commercial does not a career make.

Joe is invited to go play in a game, the Pro Bowl, and it's in Tampa. So I go down there, Mike Bite (Joe's lawyer who negotiated the famous $400,000 deal with the Jets) is down there, and I'm not kidding, he's basically camped out in Joe's room. He is a sketch. Mike is the funniest character you will ever meet in your life, a unique personality, a trusted and close personal friend and close advisor to Joe and me to this day. The Schick deal was not his, and while he was always cordial, being in Birmingham, he couldn't help but notice that my proximity to Joe in New York was positioning me to play a more important role in Joe's business life.

At that point, Mike had also gotten Joe into something called Broadway Joe's Restaurants. It was a public company, and it was starting to have some problems. And the problems now loomed as potential huge problems, not just, "Hey, you can lose some money." Now it was all of a sudden the SEC and the IRS could get involved, and this problem, and that problem. I recognized the potential liability could be significant. So it was a little bit scary.

By that time I had made it my business to become acquainted with some of the most prominent law firms in New York. Most of the companies that I had done deals with were using high-priced, top-notch lawyers, and I cultivated their friendship for future reference.

After these troubles came to light, Joe and I had a meeting back in New York. I had gotten a lot of things ready. I think this was subsequent to me doing a couple of deals, too. I was at his apartment and his date's in the other room. She was there, but I laid everything on the table to him. I told him about a lot of deals that were on the table that I had put together, and then I told him I needed to deal with his Broadway Joe's business. Always loyal to the guys that believed in him from the start, he said, "Well, you can get involved, but you can't do these things."

Then I told him what I thought of the potential liability of the Broadway Joe's situation and of how I thought we should bring in a Wall Street law firm to help get him out of the deal so that he wouldn't be left holding the bag. Joe has a shrewd business sense and an uncanny way of taking in a lot of information, processing it and making a quick but incisive decision. He heard me out and understood that he could do well for himself if he had one guy, one focal point in close proximity to evaluate deals and attend to the business half of his life in a way that made sense. That guy could bring him the deals that were the most attractive, and they could figure out which ones were the right ones to do and which ones weren't. From that point forward, that guy was me. Joe had developed a confidence in my ability to handle the deal or solve the problem or find the qualified people to solve the problem, if I felt that it was over my head.

Joe knew that endorsements and outside business deals were what would make or break him financially, but the deal had to be right. At one time, Roone

Arledge made a concerted effort to get Joe to join the *Monday Night Football* broadcast team. Roone had a young assistant, Dick Ebersol, who later went on to great success at NBC. I think I asked for $5 million at the time. Arledge was aghast. It made no difference. Joe wasn't going to quit football to don the yellow ABC jacket. No matter; several years later we picked up that payday.

Joe played football a little like the way Michelangelo painted the Sistine Chapel for the Vatican. He wasn't doing it for the money. There wasn't much money in playing pro football back then because of the stranglehold the league had on player mobility. There was no free agency, and you took what they gave you, because if you pushed too hard, you'd be out of a job. The owners owned you after the AFL-NFL merger. I think Joe kept playing football in spite of the severity of his injuries and the constant pain because it was his genius and his soul just made him do it, no matter what. And like Michelangelo, he knew that the Sistine Chapel work wasn't going to feed his family for the rest of his life. The way to pay his bills was to do some work for the Medicis. And the Medicis at this time were Arrow Shirts, Hamilton Beach, Beautymist pantyhose, La-Z-Boy chairs, Puma, etc.

Several years ago, sports memorabilia became a big thing. Some players were commanding big prices for autograph signings at sports shows. I never liked the idea. Players were doing secret deals for cash, a sure way to invite the IRS into your life. Not until the money got so big that it couldn't be ignored did I finally agree to meet the young man who had been calling for years with lucrative signing offers for Joe. So I invite this young man, Harlan Werner, to my home in New Orleans to hear his proposal. Twenty-five thousand dollars for an afternoon signing, which he claimed was the highest price at the time. My counterproposal? I really wanted to take his temperature—$750,000 for a multi-year deal. Harlan, an anti-establishment type of guy of unquestionable principles, choked at the thought of the commitment, but I convinced him that

Joe would be the best person he ever worked with. Today, many years and millions later, Harlan has become an indispensable and trusted member of our business family.

We are a lean organization. Joe and I and our longtime trusted associate Marian Gianco. We are fortunate to have talented and capable advisers who have been with us for a long time.

And then there was the World Football League and Faberge, a confluence of opportunity that would be an object lesson of when one door closes another one opens.

In the 1970s, there were no free agents. There was not even the concept of a free agent. The Jets had the rights to Joe, so nobody else could come close to him. So he either played for the Jets or he didn't play, even though his contract was up. End of story.

Meanwhile, I was trying to work out a long-term deal with Faberge. They had offered Joe a commercial for Brut Cologne. At the time, they used several big-name sports figures in their campaign, including Mickey Mantle and Willie Mays. Faberge was a glamorous company. Before Joe Namath, many young guys would never consider using hair care or grooming products. It was considered effeminate. Once Joe started endorsing cologne and showing guys that you could be cool, manly, and stylish and smell good, too, then sales went wild.

At the same time came an inquiry from Revlon. They were interested in Joe doing a commercial for their Pub cologne.

Faberge and I are in the middle of negotiating a deal, and I have lunch at the Four Seasons with some executives from Revlon to hear their proposal. Revlon makes me an offer for substantially more than the Faberge deal, but I figure I have that in the can if we can't come to an agreement with Faberge. So the Jets play a preseason game on a Friday night in Tampa Bay. John Free, the

Jets' business manager, extends me a unique privilege. He invites me to sit on the bench during the game. I do, even though I'm not really feeling comfortable about it. You can't really see anything from there, as the field is raised and the players block your view, and the other players resent seeing another player's lawyers or agents or business managers having that kind of access.

But my client, Joe Namath, is special. He was filling the stadium for preseason games, a big profit center for the franchise. I was looking forward to flying to Birmingham after the game for the premiere of Joe's movie *The Last Rebel.* Producer Larry Spangler has arranged for a private jet for us to leave right after the game. It's going to be a great weekend.

Joe throws a pass. The pass is intercepted. All of a sudden, all the guys on the sideline jump up and I can't see what's happened. I'm sitting at the end of the bench trying to be as anonymous as possible. So now all the players recede and here comes Joe hobbling toward me, and I'm like, "Whoa… I don't want any spotlight." So of course he comes toward me and sits down right next to me.

Joe is cursing, really, really cursing, and Dr. Nicholas comes and he looks down and he takes his hands behind Joe's calf and he pulls his calf. As he pulls, Joe's entire lower leg moves forward, separating at the knee like it's on an elastic band. I look at that and I'm stunned. He says, "Okay, okay Joe; we're going to have to go into New York immediately and operate. We're going to go back on the plane with the team and operate in the morning." So I go with him. This is 1971. Joe's doing okay financially, but he's not set for life by any stretch of the imagination.

I go to the hospital and Dr. Nicholas says, "Look, we'd like you to come into the operating room, because if we have to do something, we're not going to be able to reach the parents or anything. In other words, if we have to freeze this knee (basically lock the joint), we're going to have you here to see that

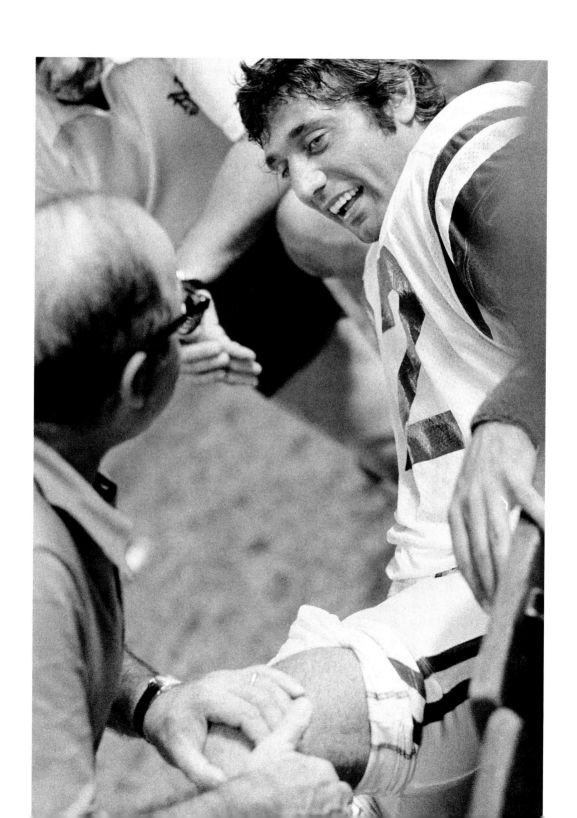

and approve that we have to do it. I'm thinking this could be the end of his career." So I'm standing in the operating room, nauseated, watching my friend's knee being cut open; Joe may never play football again. I can't screw around with Faberge. The first thing Monday morning I call and make a deal with Revlon. I do not want Joe to end up like his hero, Johnny Unitas, who is just about crippled and in the tail end of a career that forces him to keep playing to earn a paycheck.

Now, Faberge's chairman George Barry calls me and says, "You're a dishonest, no-good you-know-what and you negotiated with us in bad faith." Arch Nadler, head of the Faberge agency Nadler and Larimer, then calls me and says, "You'll never do another deal on Madison Avenue, if we have anything to do with it."

The kind of guy who uses it doesn't need it.

Pub Cologne.

After Shave, After Shave Balm, Deodorant Spray, too.
Created for men by Revlon.

Fast-forward two years: Now Joe's Jets contract is up. I have no negotiating leverage. I have become friends and made up with the guys from Faberge. I meet with Faberge's Richard Barry, the son of George Barry, who is now the president of the company. So Richard and I start doing a deal, and I say, "Look, Richard, what you really need to do is you need to sign Joe to a long-term contract. Sign Joe for 20 years for $250,000 a year, $5 million. The publicity alone will be worth a fortune to Faberge." He says, "Let's go play basketball." Jimmy Griffin and I are at his farm in New Jersey; I'm playing basketball in my bare feet with him, getting calluses. Anyhow, we make a tentative deal. Twenty years, 250 a year firm, subject to Faberge board approval.

Now all of a sudden, here comes along the World Football League. After the AFL managed to compete with the NFL and bring in competitive revenues, a lot of new professional leagues started to be put together. The goal was to compete and then merge into the established league, just like the AFL did with the NFL. Well, the guy who everyone credited with making the AFL viable was none other than Joe Namath. Joe's $400,000 deal scared the hell out of the NFL, and as the two leagues continued to escalate their bidding for players out of college, they figured out that the only people who were benefiting from the competition were the players and the fans. So naturally, they merged and returned to the status quo.

Now the World Football League starts up, and they successfully lure a lot of big-name talent to the other side. Players like Larry Csonka, Jim Kiick, Paul Warfield; even Super Bowl hero George Sauer from the Jets ends up going to the new league.

Here's a side story about George Sauer. After Joe retired from football during the Bachelor's III controversy with Pete Rozelle, a lot of players in the NFL sided with Joe. They saw the NFL as a big bully, and they weren't going to take it anymore. Anyway, George Sauer was one of these guys, and he quit.

He says "I'd rather dig ditches for a living than play for the NFL." Now, there was another guy on the Jets, Gerry Philbin, who was a fantastic defensive lineman. Gerry had grown up, like Joe and me, with little, and he had one of the greatest lines ever. After he read George's quote in the paper, he said, "Spoken like a man who never dug a ditch."

Anyway, all of the WFL's owners banded together and figured that if they could get the biggest name in pro football to sign, the box office and television revenue would follow. So I negotiated with the WFL and worked out the biggest deal for a player in that era or any era. Joe would have owned a piece of the team, a part of the league and part of the TV contract in perpetuity, about $5 million guaranteed. But I hadn't presented the deal to Joe yet.

I take the deal to Tuscaloosa, where Joe has opened up a nightclub with Mike Bite and our friend Frank Cicatiello. The next morning we're going to go somewhere. Joe's got this Lincoln convertible. So I'm telling him about this deal, and I'm looking at him feeling like I've killed the bear and brought it home, but because it rained the night before, there was water in the well of his car. He's got a bucket or some kind of coffee can to dump out the water, and I'm saying, "Joe, this is $5 million." And as I'm saying this to him, he's preoccupied with getting the water out. He doesn't care. And I'm saying to myself, because I've known him for 20 years by this point, it's not what he wants to do. He's not going to do the deal with the WFL. So now I've got the deal tentatively set with them and Joe's not interested.

We have to be in Fort Lauderdale that weekend for another Bachelor's III nightclub opening. On the way, I tell him about Faberge. Before I made the deal I asked Joe, "If I get you $5 million will you do it? Be on the hook for 20 years?" He said, "For $5 million, I'll drink the stuff."

So I have all the PR guys lined up in Fort Lauderdale and say we're going to make an announcement that Monday. So I call for a press conference at the

Four Seasons restaurant in New York, and I call in all of the chits, Howard Cosell, Roone Arledge, all the network reporters in town—everybody like that. I've got this young kid who worked for me, Jimmy Griffin, he's an agent now at William Morris, and I stick him up there on the podium with everyone. And the big announcement is not that Joe is going to go to the WFL, as everyone expects, but that he is signing a $5 million contract with Faberge. This signal to the Jets is basically, Joe doesn't have to play if he doesn't want to, and he's certainly not going to play if he doesn't get the deal he wants.

With that press conference and the major headlines in all of the newspapers that it throws off, Faberge is delighted. The WFL is furious. But now Joe has a level of security and tremendous leverage when the paper contracts show up from Faberge. He's not signing any contract with the Jets unless they give him what he wants. The bottom line is this: The Faberge deal gives us the leverage to negotiate the best deal in football at the time. And enormous publicity to boot.

Fabergé is proud to announce that
Joe Namath will be the
spokesman for Brut during its TV sponsorship
of the 1976 Olympic Games.

So, with the football, Joe got paid something—a lot for that time. I think half a million a year was the most he ever made, but it was his stardom that supported him. The celebrity business was just huge. Every guy in America wanted to be Joe Namath, and the women of America loved Joe Namath, old, young, pretty, not so pretty, thin, not so thin, white, black, they all loved Broadway Joe. Talk about demographic viability.

But the celebrity was also calculated; it wasn't the real Joe. It was a business, and because of Joe's fondness for his first big deal with Sonny Werblin, we always stayed at the Beverly Hills Hotel. One time we're staying there—in the early '70s—and Joe asks me to catch some of his passes near his cabana. So he's zinging them to me and I'm getting bruises on my hands and arms. A couple of guys walk by, looking very familiar. They have on very conservative suits, pressed white shirts and look very much like East Coast kind of businessmen. It comes to me a few hours later—John Ehrlichman, H.R. Haldeman, John Mitchell and Ron Ziegler—four of President Nixon's men who would find themselves in a lot of trouble after the Watergate break-in. I remember them looking at us funny, and when I read that Joe had been placed on Nixon's enemies list, it kind of made sense.

In each off-season, we did celebrity shows—Flip Wilson, Sonny and Cher, *Laugh-In*, and the *Dean Martin Celebrity Roasts*. Other TV appearances (one of the all-time classics and my business associate Gordon Dumont's favorite was *The Brady Bunch*) and commercials gave Joe more visibility with his helmet off than with it on on the field. Joe guest hosted a lot of talk shows, too, and had frequent appearance requests in the off-season for variety shows. He even filled in for Johnny Carson, hosting *The Tonight Show*. Most seasoned entertainers might not have been up to the task, but Joe handled it brilliantly. So much so that he got his own talk show, which lasted a couple of seasons before it became too much of a distraction.

Photo: Harry Benson

And then Joe started getting movie roles, too. There was nothing to do in the summertime, nothing to do in the off-season. Adding the movies was even better. More income, and Joe grew to enjoy acting. He made a whole bunch: *Norwood, C.C. and Company, The Last Rebel, Avalanche Express* and *Chattanooga Choo Choo.* The Hollywood experience led Joe to stage acting. Most people don't realize that Joe spent several years after his football career appearing in theatrical productions around the country. Someone once asked Joe which was harder, acting or football. "No one is trying to knock your head off in acting," was his reply.

Then there were the nightclubs—the NFL's favorite club, Bachelor's III in New York, Bachelor's III in Boston, Bachelor's III in Fort Lauderdale, and the Joe Namath clubs in Tuscaloosa and Birmingham. There are different generations for these things. Joe's first involvement was with Broadway Joe's. That fell apart and we got him out of that. Broadway Joe's was a fast-food franchise. The logic was you're going to eat somewhere, why not go to the place where you're going to have all those people come and see you and we'll be able to make some money from it? Of course, nobody was a real professional restaurateur who had a real formula for how to do it with lasting success. But we did all right. My dear friend J.D. Jordan, whose business counsel I am fortunate to have, reminds me when I run into trouble, "Experience gives the test before it teaches the lesson." I've certainly gained some experience through the years after some painful lessons.

The overriding truth of Joe Namath as a businessperson is that he is a consummate professional. He's always ready to work, and he's always got that idea of "This has to be worth it. This has to be something that I'm really invested in." You know, "I've got to be appreciated, and I've got to know what these people are doing" is the approach. And like anything else, we look to maximize our potential in each deal. We both came from a pool-hall, street-sense background, and when you come from the street you always look for whoever's out of line. When you find trouble, you deal with it and break that association. When you find something that works, you trust it. Simple as that. Classic Sports Network, CBS SportsLine, Vestin Mortgage and numerous other deals, present, past and future, continue to intrigue, edify and educate us.

So now it's Joe's last year, his contract is up and the Jets are just awful. They put Joe on waivers. Joe's going to retire, but the Los Angeles Rams, who are now owned by Carroll Rosenbloom (owner of the 1969 Colts) and coached by Chuck Knox, want him. They really need Joe. The Rams' general manager,

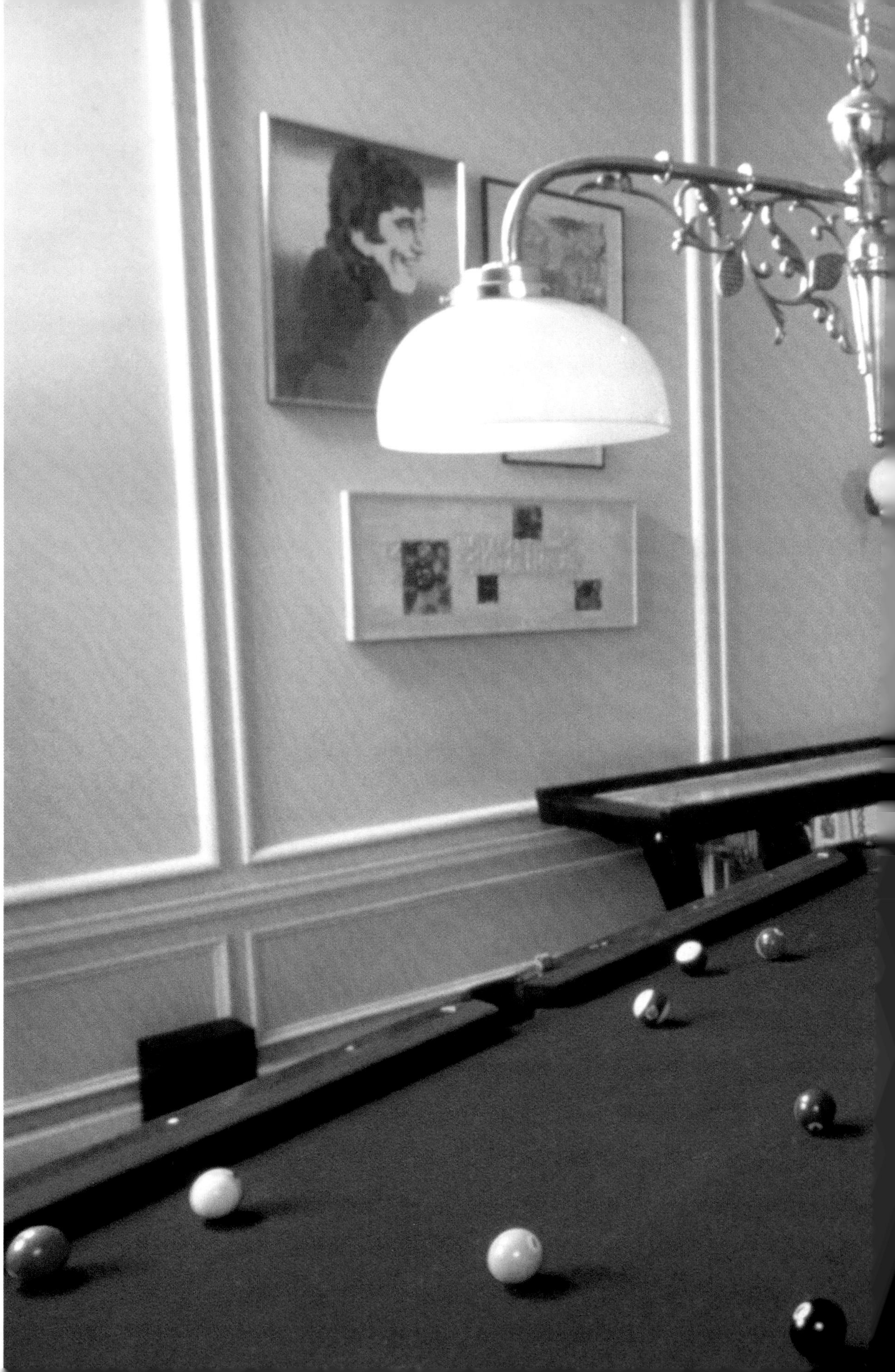

Photo: Harry Benson

Don Klosterman, says they're going to give him what he wants, and Joe's going to go play there for a year. Then it becomes, not a hard negotiation, but we're not giving in on anything and this is it; if you don't want him you don't want him. So we make our deal. Joe goes to L.A.; it's his last year. Let's just say it was a learning experience. But you know our philosophy: Any time you can learn, if you're paid for it, you should be grateful. But it ended up as probably one of the best deals for Joe.

The Rams insist that everyone must be in the best possible shape—all the players have to run for conditioning. Joe's knees won't allow it, and we explain that Joe must be exempt from running.

The Rams trainers come up with an alternative—Joe will have to swim. They put paddles on his hands and floats on his legs. They get him a swimming coach. Joe ends up swimming an hour or more every day.

I see him a month later in the locker room, and I'm amazed at how developed his shoulders and upper body have become from the swimming regimen. Ironically, football took away his mobility but gave him the cardiovascular good health and longevity through his continued swimming discipline.

Even though he became Aquaman, it was a difficult year for Joe. At the end, they benched him after a game in Chicago. What I think happened was that Rosenbloom never got over the fact that Joe beat his Colts in the Super Bowl. He owned them before he owned the Rams. He needed to get Joe Namath somehow, and a way that he could do it was with money. I think Rosenbloom sincerely believed that Joe could takes his Rams to the Super Bowl, but the problem was that Chuck Knox didn't appreciate his owner making his starting quarterback decision.

Now, Chuck also grew up in Western Pennsylvania—across the river from Beaver Falls in Sewickley—and he knew Joe from the time he played junior high school basketball. Plus, Chuck was instrumental in getting the Jets to sign Joe out of Alabama. He thought Joe was one of the greatest quarterbacks in the history of the game. But he was in a terrible position. Chuck was loyal to his starting quarterback from the previous season, Pat Haden. He had groomed him.

He stuck with Joe for four games, but then benched him for the rest of the year. I suspected Rosenbloom's frugal business sense operating behind the scenes. I kind of thought what they were doing was giving a message: "Joe, we don't want you to suit up; we want you to sit here in case we need you to suit up." That they were trying to humiliate him so that he would walk away, so they would not have to pay him. I basically told them, "Don't do that, if you try to do something like that, I'll go after you, you guys are paying."

But in the end, I don't think it was a mistake, because if you're Joe Namath and you think you still have something in you, you've got to go. If he didn't, he would always wonder, "If I had just done that one more year..." So many people go through life and they regret not doing things they could have done. Whittier said it best, so much so that it's almost a cliché now: "For of all sad words of tongue or pen, The saddest are these, 'It might have been!'"

And sometimes people's regrets are the result of not learning from their mistakes. Joe, on the other hand, is someone who learns from his mistakes and is a true student of his own life. So he knows intimately everything that he's ever done. You can ask him about things, and he remembers incredibly minute details about everything he's ever done.

What was the biggest irony about the whole Rams situation was that it could have turned out so differently. The Rams were playing the Minnesota Vikings at home in the 1977 playoffs. The Rams' quarterback, Pat Haden, was having a very bad day and the team was struggling. There was plenty of time left, and the Rams were down by a couple of touchdowns. One of the coaches

Photo: Harry Benson

asked Joe to warm up. He did and was ready to go. Everyone in that stadium and watching on television moved to the front of their seats. Joe Namath would come in and do what he always did: throw the bomb, go for broke, win the freaking game or die trying. This was going be great!

But Chuck Knox didn't see it that way. It was like Agamemnon holding back Achilles. The stage had been set, but Knox kept the star in the wings.

Now, Joe is very discerning about his commercial commitments. He's dedicated to his family, and with one young lady in college and another one in high school, he's got his hands full. He's comfortable. He's comfortable financially. He's comfortable personally. He's comfortable emotionally, and he's in a place in his life where he doesn't need to reach. He doesn't need to stretch. He's comfortable being Joe Namath. Who wouldn't be?

by Joe Namath

Sunday, November 10, 1974
Yale Bowl
New Haven, Connecticut

New York Jets at New York Giants

Coach Ewbank retired as Head Coach after the 1973 season. He had contracted Myasthenia Gravis, a debilitating neuromuscular disease that does all sorts of odd things to the control of specific muscle groups. The disease affects each person in different ways. For Weeb, he had a very hard time keeping his eyelids open. He would come to practice, and the trainer's would have to tape his eyelids up to eyebrows. The nerves just wouldn't allow those eyelids to stay up.

Weeb didn't want to retire – I mean, he was still spry and very much alert mentally. As a player who had been with him my entire pro career, seeing him go through that year was somewhat sad. But he never complained. Weeb, he'd laugh it off. He really was a brave man. And he was so tough, he ended up living longer with that disease than most thought possible.

He continued on as Jets General Manager in 1974, and he hired the former head coach of the St. Louis Cardinals and his son-in-law, Charley Winner, as the Jets new head coach. The Jets really hadn't been the same since a heartbreaking loss at Shea against eventual Super Bowl Champion Kansas City in the 1969 postseason. And in 1974, we only had six players left from the Super Bowl win.

Our mediocrity speaks for itself. **1969**: 10-5, **1970**: 4-10, **1971**: 6-8, **1972**: 7-7, **1973**: 4-10.

"Who Cares?" led the *New York Post's* pre-game coverage of the Giants-Jets meeting. That game would turn out to be the only regular season game I would play against our cross town rival. We had a grand time beating the Giants in a pre-season game 37-14 the year after the Super Bowl, but the old AFL-NFL rivalry wasn't what it once was. The merged NFL had absorbed any lingering AFL nostalgia. I mean the Baltimore Colts were in our division now.

With New York's records—Jets 1-7, Giants 2-6—the importance of this game was not lost on television network executives. NBC's Chet Simmons, then the vice president in charge of sports operations, recommended to the local NBC affiliate (WNBC) not to televise the game. The year before, WNBC's executive vice president and general manager, Art Watson, had bumped two Jet games off the tube. The next to the last game against the Colts was replaced by Kansas City-Cleveland and the last one against the Bills (Weeb's last game and the one that sent O.J. Simpson over the 2,000 yard mark for rushing in a season) was bumped for Denver-Oakland. One exec commented, "What it boils down to is this: do you want to see winners or do you want to see losers?"

Ironically, they stopped televising our games two weeks previously, a Jets-Colts Shea Stadium sellout on October 20, 1974. Local affiliates had the ultimate decision about whether to broadcast the home team or not if a sell-out had occurred. But by this time, unlike the *Heidi* game, there were few switchboard complaints from Jets fans when WNBC elected "not." And certainly, no telephone circuits blew out.

We were in such a funk that I stopped talking to reporters after a 24-0 loss against the Patriots. "The way the situation is, I can see nothing productive about talking to them right now."

The Giants weren't ripping up the league either. I mean they still had Pete Gogolak playing for them. Giant Owner Wellington Mara signed away Gogolak from Buffalo back in 1966, the deal that started the whole AFL-NFL merger in the first place. In rebuild mode ever since, the 1974 Giants played home games at the Yale Bowl in New Haven, Connecticut. A few years before, the New Jersey Sports and Exhibition Authority's Chairman, Mr. David A. "Sonny" Werblin, convinced Mr. Mara to leave Yankee Stadium. If Mr. Mara committed to a football only, state-of-the-art facility, erected in a New Jersey swamp called The Meadowlands, the man who created the Jets would agree to call it "Giants Stadium."

But until the future was ready, the Giants used Walter Camp's old field—a crumbling edifice with nineteenth-century locker rooms. Old school? I wouldn't have been surprised if the Giants came out in leather helmets. Before the game, one of our players was quoted as saying, "I played four years in high school, four years in college and a few years in the pros and all that rah-rah stuff just rolls off my back. I get myself up for the games. I don't need anybody to do it for me."

We just weren't very good. We didn't have a lot of talent, and we hadn't performed well as a team. But to me, the game was colossal. When I started pro ball (the clock started the moment I woke in Lenox Hill Hospital after surgery #1), I thanked God for the possibility of playing four years. In the bus to the Yale Bowl, I was 31 years old, with nine years under my belt. No one would have bet I'd still be around. The finest medical opinions on the planet didn't expect me to make it beyond 1969, and here I was playing in Walter Camp's back yard against the New York Giants. It was wonderful.

Sure, we might lose the game. We might lose every game from that point forward. But the great thing about football—one of them—is that there is always honor, win or lose. Dick Butkus never got to the playoffs. But he defines the linebacker position even today. And I've never heard anyone call Dick Butkus a loser.

But I did know what my teammate was talking about. I wasn't a rookie. If you play enough games, it can be difficult to get as enthused as you might have in earlier years. We played the Cowboys in 1971, and in the first quarter, they were leading 28-nothing. We had had the ball twice, now they had it, and things looked real bad. We ended up losing 52-10. When you're down 28-nothing to the Dallas Cowboys at Texas Stadium in the first quarter, you can't help but lose some of the ol' enthusiasm. You take a deep breath and think, "Man, this is gonna be tough." But still, you know you've got to go out there and try your best. It's not like I'm gonna quit. You just gotta adjust your game plan a bit.

Before the game, we had a players-only, air-clearing meeting. As leaders of the Jets old guard—a role I still cherish today—a few of us felt it was up to us to get the players fired up again. Emerson Boozer spoke first, then Ralph Baker, two critical players in Jets history. The young guys really didn't get it. We were playing in nowhere with no TV cameras against a 2-6 team.

I remember that game clearly.

We had the ball four times in the first half and we scored twice—a touchdown and a field goal. The first drive was a thing of beauty. We hit seven straight passes and David Knight, a second year man with terrific hands, caught a 19-yarder in the end zone for our first touchdown.

The Giants were as up for this game as we were. Their quarterback, Craig Morton, drove the Giant offense efficiently and methodically to three scores in the first half—two field goals by Pete Gogolak and a touchdown pass to Bob Tucker. At the half, Giants 13, Jets 10.

The second half began with one of the longest sustained drives in my career. Reminiscent of the six-minute plus drive that sealed our win against the Kansas City Chiefs in 1968; we held the ball for close to ten and a half minutes and kicked a field goal to tie it at 13.

The Giants answered quickly. Morton was hot and led them to a touchdown on a 12-yard pass to Bob Grim. Giants 20, Jets 13.

The fourth quarter opened with another Jet drive. We mixed up the run with short passes and got to third and inches deep in Giant territory. Now the last thing anyone would expect would be a quarterback sneak—I mean, from me? So I ran it and we got the first down. Five plays later we were on the 3-yard line. In the huddle, I had called an off tackle run with Boo (34 Power). When I came to the line, I saw that the Giants were in a 6-1 goal-line defense. Their talented rookie linebacker, Brad Van Pelt, who would have containment responsibilities on the backside of our called play, was cheating inside. He was going to come hard!

"I hit the hole and stopped," remembered Boo. "I don't have the ball and I'm figuring it must've been a bad exchange between me and Joe. I hear the crowd roar and I look up and see the son of a gun going into the end zone."

Without telling anyone, I kept the ball myself on a bootleg.

David Knight said, "It must have taken him ten seconds to go five yards… He could have gotten killed."

Now people assumed that my herky-jerky running form was from my bad knees. But in fact, it was the freak waterskiing accident that severed hamstring muscles that was responsible for the exaggerated length of time it took me to run the bootleg. When your hamstring is bad, you just can't extend your leg and take a full running stride. I crossed the goal line, we kicked he extra point, and we were tied 20-20.

The final eight minutes of the game were an emotional roller coaster. The Giants came back and drove to our 30-yard line, but defensive lineman Mark Lomas killed their drive with a sack of Morton that took them out of field goal range.

The teams exchanged punts, and with 3:02 left, we got the ball and drove it down to the Giant 17 with 16 seconds to go. Pat Leahy came in for the winning field goal attempt. Pat would go on to be one of the most reliable kickers of the era, but this was his first professional football game. He was a soccer player before joining the Jets and was one of the first to perfect the soccer style kick.

Unfortunately, he kicked the ball right into our center John Schmitt's rear end. They credited the Giants' Jim Steinke with a block, but it was pretty clear to the players that the ball just didn't have enough height. Especially Schmitt.

The game went into sudden death overtime.

The Giants won the coin toss. They drove to our 32 but our defense stopped them and the Giants brought in Pete Gogolak for the field goal to win it. The ghost of the AFL must have pushed the ball wide, because Pete missed.

We got the ball and when I came to the line of scrimmage, I was going to go to WR Jerome Barkum, lined up outside. But when I saw the cornerbacks rolling up in double-double coverage on our wide outs, I looked for TE Rich Caster. Caster went down the middle on a post route and I hit him for a 42-yard gain. We were on the Giant 33. Four plays later we were in a second and goal from the 5. After Pat missed the chip shot at the end of regulation, we were intent on getting the ball over the goal line. Ken Shipp, our offensive coordinator, sent Boo in with a play action pass. Boo went into the line as if he were blocking for our fullback Bob Burns. He would then peel off from linebacker Brad Van Pelt to the left side of the end zone.

"Van Pelt is on me and if he plays me as a blocker, I know I've got him. I can just slide off and catch the pass. But he didn't. He played pass the entire time." Boozer recalled.

But ol' Boo managed to slip by Van Pelt and he caught the touchdown pass with 8:16 seconds left in overtime. The New York Jets notched the first regular season sudden-death win in NFL history.

Giant Head Coach Bill Arnsparger came into the Jet locker room after the game and shook my hand.

"Helluva job," he said. "There hasn't been many times where I've felt that way. Great game."

I looked him in the eye and said "Thank you, sir."

1960 Season	
Wins	9
Losses	0
Ties	0
Passing Completions	85
Passing Attempts	146
Passing Yard	1564
Passing Touchdowns	12
Passing Interceptions	1
Longest Pass	60
Rushing Attempts	28
Rushing Yards	259
Rushing Touchdowns	5

BEAVER FALLS HIGH SCHOOL TIGERS

1962 Season	
Wins	10
Losses	1
Ties	0
Passing Completions	85
Passing Attempts	163
Passing Yard	1278
Passing Touchdowns	14
Passing Interceptions	8
Longest Pass	52
Rushing Attempts	91
Rushing Yards	253
Rushing Touchdowns	4

UNIVERSITY OF ALABAMA CRIMSON TIDE

1963 Season	
Wins	9
Losses	2
Ties	0
Passing Completions	64
Passing Attempts	128
Passing Yard	765
Passing Touchdowns	8
Passing Interceptions	7
Longest Pass	47
Rushing Attempts	76
Rushing Yards	211
Rushing Touchdowns	5

UNIVERSITY OF ALABAMA CRIMSON TIDE

1964 Season

12

UNIVERSITY OF ALABAMA
CRIMSON TIDE

Wins	10
Losses	1
Ties	0
Passing Completions	82
Passing Attempts	137
Passing Yard	1012
Passing Touchdowns	8
Passing Interceptions	5
Longest Pass	45
Rushing Attempts	46
Rushing Yards	134
Rushing Touchdowns	6

JOE NAMATH
QUARTERBACK

1965 Season

NEW YORK
JETS

Wins	5
Losses	8
Ties	1
Passing Completions	164
Passing Attempts	340
Passing Yard	2220
Passing Touchdowns	18
Passing Interceptions	15
Longest Pass	62
Rushing Attempts	8
Rushing Yards	19
Rushing Touchdowns	0

1966 Season

NEW YORK
JETS

Wins	6
Losses	6
Ties	2
Passing Completions	232
Passing Attempts	471
Passing Yard	3379
Passing Touchdowns	19
Passing Interceptions	27
Longest Pass	77
Rushing Attempts	6
Rushing Yards	42
Rushing Touchdowns	2

1967 Season

NEW YORK
JETS

Wins	8
Losses	5
Ties	1
Passing Completions	258
Passing Attempts	491
Passing Yard	4007
Passing Touchdowns	26
Passing Interceptions	28
Longest Pass	75
Rushing Attempts	6
Rushing Yards	14
Rushing Touchdowns	0

1968 Season

NEW YORK
JETS

Wins	13
Losses	3
Ties	0
Passing Completions	187
Passing Attempts	380
Passing Yard	3147
Passing Touchdowns	15
Passing Interceptions	17
Longest Pass	87
Rushing Attempts	5
Rushing Yards	11
Rushing Touchdowns	2

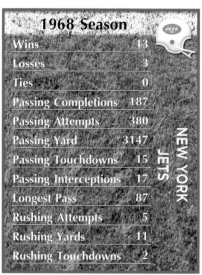

1969 Season — NEW YORK JETS

Wins	10
Losses	4
Ties	0
Passing Completions	185
Passing Attempts	361
Passing Yard	2734
Passing Touchdowns	19
Passing Interceptions	17
Longest Pass	60
Rushing Attempts	11
Rushing Yards	33
Rushing Touchdowns	2

1970 Season — NEW YORK JETS

Wins	4
Losses	10
Ties	0
Passing Completions	90
Passing Attempts	179
Passing Yard	1259
Passing Touchdowns	5
Passing Interceptions	12
Longest Pass	72
Rushing Attempts	1
Rushing Yards	-1
Rushing Touchdowns	0

1971 Season — NEW YORK JETS

Wins	6
Losses	8
Ties	0
Passing Completions	28
Passing Attempts	59
Passing Yard	537
Passing Touchdowns	5
Passing Interceptions	6
Longest Pass	74
Rushing Attempts	3
Rushing Yards	-1
Rushing Touchdowns	0

1972 Season — NEW YORK JETS

Wins	7
Losses	7
Ties	0
Passing Completions	162
Passing Attempts	324
Passing Yard	2816
Passing Touchdowns	19
Passing Interceptions	21
Longest Pass	80
Rushing Attempts	6
Rushing Yards	8
Rushing Touchdowns	0

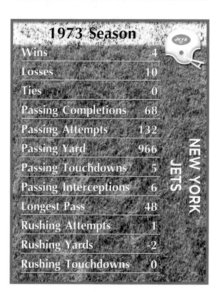

1973 Season — NEW YORK JETS

Wins	4
Losses	10
Ties	0
Passing Completions	68
Passing Attempts	132
Passing Yard	966
Passing Touchdowns	5
Passing Interceptions	6
Longest Pass	48
Rushing Attempts	1
Rushing Yards	-2
Rushing Touchdowns	0

1974 Season — NEW YORK JETS

Wins	7
Losses	7
Ties	0
Passing Completions	191
Passing Attempts	360
Passing Yard	2616
Passing Touchdowns	20
Passing Interceptions	22
Longest Pass	89
Rushing Attempts	8
Rushing Yards	1
Rushing Touchdowns	1

1975 Season — NEW YORK JETS

Wins	3
Losses	11
Ties	0
Passing Completions	157
Passing Attempts	325
Passing Yard	2287
Passing Touchdowns	15
Passing Interceptions	28
Longest Pass	56
Rushing Attempts	10
Rushing Yards	6
Rushing Touchdowns	0

1976 Season — NEW YORK JETS

Wins	3
Losses	11
Ties	0
Passing Completions	114
Passing Attempts	230
Passing Yard	1090
Passing Touchdowns	4
Passing Interceptions	16
Longest Pass	37
Rushing Attempts	2
Rushing Yards	5
Rushing Touchdowns	0

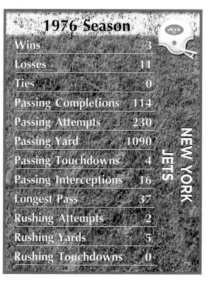

1977 Season — LOS ANGELES RAMS

Wins	10
Losses	4
Ties	0
Passing Completions	50
Passing Attempts	107
Passing Yard	606
Passing Touchdowns	3
Passing Interceptions	5
Longest Pass	37
Rushing Attempts	4
Rushing Yards	5
Rushing Touchdowns	0

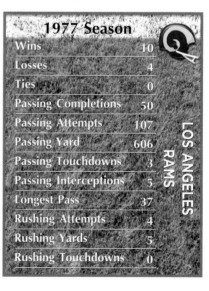

Career Totals

Games Played	182
Wins	103
Losses	75
Ties	4
Passing Completions	2252
Passing Attempts	4450
Passing Yard	32914
Passing Touchdowns	218
Passing Interceptions	245
Longest Pass	89
Rushing Attempts	312
Rushing Yards	997
Rushing Touchdowns	27

Photo Credits

12